Religion & Society

Sarah K. Tyler
Gordon Reid

Philip Allan Updates
Market Place
Deddington
Oxfordshire
OX15 0SE

Tel: 01869 338652
Fax: 01869 337590
e-mail: sales@philipallan.co.uk
www.philipallan.co.uk

ISBN-13: 978-1-84489-222-8
ISBN-10: 1-84489-222-0

Design by Neil Fozzard

Printed by Scotprint, Haddington

Environmental information
The paper on which this title is printed is sourced from managed, sustainable forests.

Contents

Introduction

This book gives you the information you need to do well in your Edexcel Religious Studies GCSE exam on religion and society. It deals with all six topic areas in Unit H: Religion and society based on a study of Christianity and at least one other religion — in this case, Islam. The six topic areas are:

- religion and social responsibility
- religion and the environment
- religion: peace and conflict
- religion: crime and punishment
- religion and medical issues (can be examined or covered by coursework)
- religion and science (can be examined or covered by coursework)

These correspond exactly with what you will find in the specification and appear in the same order in this book as they do in the specification.

The exam

In your exam you will have to answer either four or five questions, depending on whether you are offering coursework. Each of the first four questions is worth 20 marks and is broken down into four parts, worth 2, 6, 8 and 4 marks respectively.

- The 2-mark question usually asks for a definition of a key term or idea.
- The 6-mark question asks you to show your knowledge of a belief or issue.
- The 8-mark question aims to see how well you understand the issues and beliefs.
- The 4-mark question asks you to consider a point of view and weigh up arguments for and against it, giving your own opinion in a carefully considered way.

If you are not doing coursework, you will have to answer a fifth question in the exam, which requires longer answers. The question is broken down into three parts, worth 4, 8 and 8 marks.

- The 4-mark question is knowledge based and asks you for information and facts about the topic.

- The first 8-mark question asks you to show your understanding of the topic.
- The second 8-mark question is evaluative — again suggesting a point of view and asking you to analyse it and make a balanced judgement.

You need to work quickly in the exam as there is a lot to cover. If you offer the fifth specification area in the exam, instead of doing coursework, remember that you are being tested for quality of writing as well as content.

Coursework

If you opt for the coursework option, you will be answering a similar set of questions to those you will find in the exam, but you will need to write more and go into more depth. The specification suggests 1,500 words for a piece of coursework, although you can, of course, write more than that. The coursework questions are broken down into two parts, again worth 20 marks overall.

- Part (a) consists of three sub-questions which are knowledge- and understanding-based and worth 12 marks.
- Part (b) consists of one 8-mark evaluation question, as in the exam.

You are likely to get plenty of guidance from your teacher about coursework. Don't rush it at the last minute — take time to perfect it and include some information that no one else in your class has in theirs. There is a lot of coursework out there and you need to make sure yours stands out.

Using this book

There are six sections in this book, each of which follows the same basic format. The main part of each section provides you with the information you need to answer questions on the topic, including definitions of key words. Most sections include quotations from religious texts and other sources, and you should aim to learn a few of these for each specification area.

Each section covers a range of views on the topic. This is important: to get top marks you must show that you are aware of and can discuss differences in belief on even some of the most central issues in religion, regardless of whether you yourself agree or disagree.

At the end of each section there is a range of questions and activities:

- **Sample questions and answers.** The questions included here represent the type of questions you will have to answer in the exam. The answers given are longer than you are likely to write in the exam, but they show you the best type of answer you could give.
- **Further questions.** These provide more examples of the type of question you will have to answer in the exam. You should use them for exam practice.
- **Class activities.** These are intended to be done in class under your teacher's guidance. Your teacher will supply you with any materials you need to complete these activities and organise you into pairs or groups as appropriate.
- **Homework.** These tasks are intended to be carried out at home. Some require access to the internet.

At the end of this book there is a glossary and a list of useful websites:

- **Glossary.** This contains all the key words and definitions found throughout the book. Use this for reference and as a revision aid.
- **Useful websites.** These are sites which you may find it helpful to refer to during your course. Some are very specific, others are more general.

Religion and social responsibility

How do Christians make moral decisions?

Christians believe God is the ultimate source of good and that, when making decisions about what is right and wrong, they should follow God's teachings and obey his will. Christians believe God makes moral commands, all of which are good, which they should accept and follow. To be a Christian means living life according to God's moral code, which is found in the **Bible** and taught by the **Church**.

There are four main ways in which Christians can make moral decisions. Some may use only one or two of them, but most will use a combination of all four:

Key words

Bible
The holy book of Christianity

Church
The Christian community. It is also used to refer to a Christian place of worship

- reading and obeying the teachings in the Bible
- following the teachings of the Church
- following their **conscience**
- using **situation ethics** to decide what is the most loving thing to do in a given situation

The authority of the Bible

Key words

Conscience
The part of the mind where a sense of right and wrong is developed

Decalogue
The Ten Commandments, found in Exodus 20 in the Bible

Situation ethics
A method of deciding right from wrong by considering what is the most loving thing to do

The Bible is the Christian holy book and Christians believe it is the word of God. In fact, it is a collection of 66 books, written over hundreds of years. It is divided into two parts: the Old Testament and the New Testament. The Old Testament was written before the time of Jesus and contains the Ten Commandments (the **Decalogue**) and the Law of Moses (the Torah). The New Testament is concerned with the life and teaching of Jesus, whom Christians believe was the Son of God — or God in human form. He came to teach humanity about the love and goodness of God and to die on the cross in order to restore the relationship between humanity and God.

For Christians, the Bible carries great authority and is the most important guide for decision making. The moral teaching of the Bible has become the basis of the legal systems in many of the countries of the Western world. The most famous of these moral teachings are the Ten Commandments (Exodus 20:1–17) and the Sermon on the Mount (Matthew 5–7), but there is a wealth of ethical and moral teaching in other books of the Bible.

Christians believe the Bible is the authentic word of God and great care has been taken over the centuries to preserve the words and meaning of the Bible. Christians believe the writers of the Bible were 'inspired' by God — that is, their words came in some way from God himself. Some believe God gave the words directly to the writers, while others believe God influenced what was written and that the writers were responsible to some degree for interpreting those words.

> God is the author of Sacred Scripture because he has inspired its human authors.
>
> (Catechism of the Catholic Church)

Not all Christians understand the Bible in quite the same way:

- Literalists believe in the exact and literal translation of the Bible and say every word of scripture is true.
- Fundamentalists say the Bible is completely inspired by God and does not contain any errors.
- Conservatives and Liberals believe the Bible was inspired by God and contains spiritual truths, but the writers, although guided by God, were writing about the social situations of the time and their teachings need to be updated to keep them relevant to today's society.
- Evangelicals see the Bible as the source of guidance on all matters of faith and behaviour.

Christians believe the Bible is the word of God

Inevitably, Christians clash over these different ways of understanding the status of the Bible. An Evangelical Christian will have different views about abortion from a Liberal, and it is difficult for the two sides to see the value of each other's position. Evangelicals and Fundamentalists worry about how God's word is treated and the effect this has on society and on the Church. Liberal Christians worry that if the teaching of the Bible is not made directly relevant to today's world, Christianity will lose support from those who think it is out of touch and lacking in compassion. It is virtually impossible to reconcile these different positions and they can often lead to extreme teachings on moral issues.

Despite these differences about how to interpret and apply the Bible's teaching, all Christians believe that God and Jesus are at the heart of the Bible, and that it can help them to learn more about God and how he wants them to lead their lives. It gives them moral guidance in the way they should live.

The authority of the Church

Many Christians read the Bible as part of their daily lives and use it to help them pray and worship God. But Christians are not left to study and work out the meaning of the Bible alone, although such private Bible study is important. They gain help from the church to which they belong and the Church itself has great authority over the lives of Christians. Christians learn much about how God wishes them to lead their lives by going to church and listening to sermons of their priest (a sermon is an explanation of the teachings in the Bible). The priest is an expert on what the Bible means and how to understand and apply the teaching within it. Christians may also meet together in their church and read the Bible in study groups to help each other understand the message of God.

Pope John Paul II (1920–2005)

As well as the teachings of their local church, Christians can discover how to lead their lives according to God's will by looking at the teachings of the Christian Church as a whole. Each denomination has authority over its members throughout the world and has its own teachings that apply to all its members. For example, within the Catholic Church, the pope and the Council of Bishops offer moral guidance through the Catechism or from the official letters of the pope, called encyclicals. In contrast, the Church of England has an elected assembly to guide its members, called the General Synod. Moreover, there are universal teachings that all Christian Churches accept, such as the Creeds, which are statements of belief that sum up the main teachings of Christian faith. For example, the Nicene Creed and the Apostles' Creed explain what Christians believe about God, Jesus and the Holy Spirit.

The role of conscience

Conscience is a way in which people, both religious and non-religious, can judge their moral actions. It is the inner part of a person where the sense of what is right and wrong is developed. The role of conscience in making moral decisions is significant and 'conscientious objections' have an important influence on society. For example, although abortions can be obtained legally, doctors are not compelled to carry out abortions if their conscience tells them that abortions are morally wrong. Some pacifists — religious and non-religious — who refuse to fight in war are called 'conscientious objectors'.

> In the depths of his conscience, man detects a law which he does not impose upon himself, but which holds him to obedience.
>> (Gaudium et Spes, a statement by the pope in 1965)

> A human being must always obey the certain judgement of his conscience.
>> (Catechism of the Catholic Church)

Christians claim everyone has a conscience, whether they believe in God or not. Conscience is given by God, but because humans have disobeyed God, conscience is imperfect and can only be made right by believing in Jesus.

> Pray for us. We are sure that we have a clear conscience and desire to live honourably in every way.
>> (Hebrews 13:18)

However, conscience needs to be instructed and trained, and the more right choices people make, the more they will be naturally inclined to the right choice every time. Thomas Aquinas said that the conscience was the moral judge and the way in which humans exercised their reason in working out what was right. It would eventually lead humans to follow God's moral law.

For the Christian, therefore, conscience is not a perfect guide as to what is right or wrong, but a useful measuring tool. J. V. Langmead Casserly writes: 'A well-trained conscience remains a factor of the utmost importance in the moral life.'

Situation ethics

Joseph Fletcher coined the phrase 'situation ethics' in the 1960s. He believed that our moral lives were based too much on obeying rules we did not understand or agree with. He thought a better basis for moral decisions was to use the principle of love. Situation ethics relies on the principle of doing the most loving thing that the situation demands. It is based on the simple teachings of Jesus: 'My command is this: Love each other as I have loved you'

(John 15:12). Fletcher believed that a person should only obey the Bible or the Church if its teaching resulted in the most loving thing to do.

> Love the Lord your God with all your heart, and with all your soul, and with all your strength and with all your mind: and love your neighbour as yourself.
>
> (Luke 10:27)

Fletcher said that love is the one principle that can be applied in every situation. He also said that love meant there could no longer be rules such as 'never' or 'always' and that people should be put first. Fletcher was precise about the kind of love that should be applied — agape love. Agape love makes it possible for people to love their enemies and to act in loving ways towards those who have not done anything to deserve that love.

Another supporter of situation ethics was J. A. T. Robinson, who wrote the influential book, *Honest to God* (1963). He believed that human beings no longer needed to be guided by moral laws to make the right decision. He wrote: 'Whatever the pointers of the law to the demands of love, there can for the Christian be no "packaged" moral judgements — for persons are more important even than "standards".' He and Fletcher suggested that the way in which Jesus treated people during his ministry was the right way, and that the Church had got too caught up in rules that ignored the needs of individuals. The way in which Jesus healed lepers, saved the adulterous woman from being stoned to death, and was prepared to break the Sabbath rules if people were helped by doing so, showed situation ethics in action.

Strengths of situation ethics

- Individual cases are judged on their own merits.
- Love seeks the wellbeing of others, even if the course of action is not the easiest one.
- It is based on the teaching of Jesus.

Weaknesses of situation ethics

- To say no rules apply, and then to say the only rule is love, is a contradiction.
- The theory depends on guessing at the consequences. It is impossible to be accurate.

- The theory justifies adultery, murder and other actions that are traditionally thought to be wrong if they occur in the interests of love.

- If people can choose to disregard God's commands simply because they feel it will be the loving thing to do, anyone can do anything they choose if they feel the good results justify disobeying God.

- It is easy to apply situation ethics in extreme cases where there is no law to cover the situation, but it is not so easy to justify its use to address everyday situations for which there are already many sources of moral guidance.

The electoral system in the UK

The UK is a representative **democracy**. This means that although there is a monarch, the country is governed by parliament. Members of parliament are elected by the adult population, all of whom have rights and freedoms — such as freedom of speech, religion and the right to vote. An **electoral system** is one which citizens vote at an election for the people they want to represent their interests and make decisions on their behalf. A general election is held every 5 years, in which people vote to decide which party will form the next government. It is important to vote because those elected to represent the people make decisions on major issues that affect everyone's lives, such as health, education, defence and taxation. If people did not vote, the country would cease to be a democracy and could become a dictatorship, in which citizens have no say in how the country is run.

Key words

Democracy
A society that has free elections and gives all its adult citizens the chance to vote on who they want to govern them

Electoral system
The way in which voting at an election is organised

The Houses of Parliament

Parliament itself, which is located in Westminster in London, is divided into two houses: the House of Commons, where the elected MPs sit; and the House of Lords, whose members are not elected. Members of the House of

Lords include former MPs and bishops. In the past, people could inherit a seat in the House of Lords. Seats in the House of Commons are given to members of parliament (MPs) who have been elected to parliament by the people in their constituency. Most MPs belong to a recognised political party. The three main parties in the UK are the Labour Party, the Conservative Party and the Liberal Democrat Party. However, there are also other less represented parties, which usually reflect a specific point of view, such as the British National Party or the Green Party. Any individual can stand for parliament in a general or local election if he or she can pay the necessary deposit. However, there is so much competition from the established parties that it would be unusual for an individual to gain enough support in a constituency to beat the representatives of the established parties.

A constituency usually comprises about 65,000 people. At a general election, candidates for the established parties stand in each constituency alongside those representing more marginal parties and any independents. On election day, the electorate — that is, everybody over 18 who is eligible to vote — goes to a polling station where they put a cross on the paper next to the name of the person they want to elect as their MP. In each constituency, the candidate who gets the highest number of votes is elected to be the member of parliament. This is called the **first-past-the-post** system.

On election day voters put their slips in the ballot box

Some people argue that this electoral system is unfair because the individual candidate who gains the most votes wins the seat, even if collectively more votes were cast against him or her. For example, if there were three candidates and the Labour candidate got 20,000 votes, the Conservative 15,000 and the Liberal Democrat 10,000, the Labour candidate would be elected as the MP even though more people (25,000) voted for the other parties. It can mean that a political party can gain millions of votes, but have no MPs. Similarly, a party can be elected to form a government even if the majority of people voted against it in the country as a whole.

MPs are responsible for representing the people of their constituencies until the next general election. As well as going to parliament in Westminster, MPs hold surgeries in their constituencies where they meet local people and deal with local issues.

When all the MPs have been elected, the party whose members have won the most seats forms the **national government** and runs the country. The leader of the winning party becomes the prime minister and selects MPs from their party to form the **cabinet**. The cabinet is the inner circle of ministers who work alongside the prime minister to run the country. Important members of the cabinet include the chancellor of the exchequer (who maintains the country's finances), the home secretary and the foreign secretary. Other cabinet ministers look after particular departments such as defence, health, employment and education.

National government has responsibility for a wide range of issues, including defence, health, social security, education, employment, transport and the environment. The government raises the money it needs to run the country through taxes, which are paid by individual taxpayers, businesses and other groups. This money, which runs to billions of pounds per year, is used to pay for hospitals, schools, the armed services, the police and social security, as well as many other public services. The day-to-day running of all these different departments is carried out by the Civil Service.

The national government is responsible for running the country as a whole. However, where small, local issues are involved, there is another system called **local government**. The country is divided into a number of districts and each has its own local council. It may also have a district council and a parish council.

Key words

Cabinet
The group of senior ministers who help the prime minister make important decisions concerning the running of the country

First-past-the-post
The voting system used in the UK to decide who is elected to be the member of parliament for each constituency. The winner is the person with the most votes

Local government
Government at a local level. This refers to local, district and parish councils which are responsible for local matters such as education

National government
The government of the whole country, led by the prime minister

Proportional representation
The voting system that looks at the proportion of votes each party gets and distributes seats in line with that percentage. For example, a party with 25% of the votes gets 25% of the seats

The members of the council are elected in the same way as MPs and the party with the most councillors forms the local council, under the leadership of a mayor.

Local government is responsible for local issues. It uses the money that national government has provided to run local schools, the police, the fire brigade, refuse collection and council housing. Money for local government is also provided by local people, who have to pay a council tax.

Scotland and Wales have their own local or regional parliaments called assemblies. These are headed by first ministers with their own cabinets which run local matters in those regions. The members of the assemblies are elected by a system called **proportional representation**. The number of seats a party wins depends on what percentage of the electorate's vote it gets. For example, if one party gets 50% of the votes, it wins half the total number of seats for its members.

Proportional representation is regarded by many as being fairer than the first-past-the-post system because it gives a more accurate reflection of the wishes of the voters. It often requires parties to work together to form a government (called a coalition). However, it means that constituencies have to be larger and this makes it difficult for MPs to deal with local matters because they represent a party rather than a group of local people. Coalitions also tend to produce weak and indecisive governments.

Finally, the UK elects people to represent the country in the European parliament. Members of the European parliament (MEPs) are elected by proportional representation.

The main political parties in the UK

There are three main political parties in the UK, together with many smaller ones. The main parties all accept the principles of democracy and national government, but differ in how they believe the country should be run. In a general election, each party puts forward to the people its own views on what it would do if it were elected to power. These views are called policies and are contained in a document called a manifesto. Broadly speaking, the main parties offer the following views.

The Labour Party

- The state (the public sector) should help the poorest members of society.
- The state should provide healthcare and education for everyone equally.
- Changes should be made to the constitution to make the government more democratic (for example, by reforming the House of Lords).

The Conservative Party

- The state should encourage people to look after themselves and take responsibility for their own lives, for example by paying for private pensions, healthcare and education. This is the private sector.
- The state should only provide what the private sector cannot supply.
- There should be little or no change to the constitution.

The Liberal Democrat Party

- The public and private sectors should work together to help everyone.
- Most responsibilities should be moved away from national government and given to local government.
- There should be reform to allow elections by proportional representation.

Christians who believe they should be involved in politics

Some Christians believe it is impossible to separate religion and politics because both are crucial aspects of life. They feel Christians have a moral responsibility to vote for the political parties that offer the policies which are most in line with the teachings of the Bible. Many Christians are directly involved in politics, either as members of parliament or as government employees.

Archbishop Desmond Tutu

Historically, Christians have always been involved in politics. In the nineteenth century, the great Christian reformer Lord Shaftesbury campaigned against the awful working conditions in British factories and the lack of education and healthcare for the children of poor families. William Wilberforce campaigned against the slave trade. More recently, the Christian leader Archbishop Desmond Tutu has campaigned against racism and apartheid in South Africa.

Key words

Faith without works
The idea that having religious faith on its own is not enough and it needs to be accompanied by good works

Justice
Maintaining what is fair, right and equal to all

Law
The rules that govern the smooth-running of human relationships in society

Many Christians believe that Jesus himself was concerned about issues that are associated today with politics. In the Sermon on the Mount, Jesus taught: 'You cannot serve both God and money' (Matthew 6:24), while in Mark 11:15–17, Jesus involved himself directly in Jewish politics when he wrecked the temple market. This market sold animals for sacrifice at expensive prices and the moneychangers charged high rates. Worshippers going to the temple, therefore, had to pay a high price to make a sacrifice or an offering to God, and Jesus condemned this:

> He overturned the tables of the moneychangers and the benches of those selling doves, and would not allow anyone to carry merchandise through the temple courts. And as he taught them, he said, 'Is it not written: "My house will be called a house of prayer for all nations"?
>
> But you have made it a "den of robbers".'
>
> (Mark 11:16–17)

Some Christians argue that it is important to have a government that puts the will of God before power, money and self-interest. This might mean, for example, having a government that spends money on things that do good for society, such as hospitals and schools, rather than one that allows wealthy people and companies to grow richer.

> Do not store up for yourselves treasures on earth, where moth and rust destroy, and where thieves break in and steal. But store up for yourselves treasure in heaven.
>
> (Matthew 6:19–20)

A nun feeds a baby who is HIV positive

The Bible also talks about the importance of people performing good actions. It is not sufficient to say you have faith in God. **Faith without works** and good actions is of little use. Christians argue that they should try to make the government act in a good and morally correct way. This means ensuring that the government respects human rights, cares for the elderly, the poor and the needy, and has a fair system of **justice**, **law** and order.

What good is it, my brothers, if a man claims to have faith but has no deeds? Can such faith save him? Suppose a brother or sister is without clothes and daily food. If one of you says to him, 'Go, I wish you well: keep warm and well fed,' but does nothing about his physical needs, what good is it? In the same way, faith by itself, if it is not accompanied by action, is dead.

(James 2:14–17)

The Churches also teach about concern for politics and suggest that Christians should be involved in helping the poor and suffering and should work for peace and a fairer division of the world's resources. In a report called *Faith in the City*, the Church of England highlighted the need for governments to be concerned with the poor and needy in the towns and cities:

God…is also to be found, despite all appearances, in the apparent waste lands of our inner cities and housing estates: that men and women are created to glorify God in and through his creation and to serve fellow human beings in the power of his love.

The Catholic Church adopts a similar view. In a statement made in 1988, the pope said:

The Church exists 'to proclaim good news to the poor and freedom for the oppressed'. It takes Christ's words 'as you did it to the least of my brethren you did it to me', not just on a personal level, but also a social one.

(Sollicitudo Rei Socialis)

In a report called *Christianity and Social Progress*, the Catholic Church called its members to action to achieve 'the common good [which] means all those conditions of human living, economic, political, cultural…make it possible for women and men to achieve the perfection of their humanity.'

Individual Christians have sometimes even gone so far as to suggest that evil and corrupt governments should be challenged and, if necessary, overthrown. Dietrich Bonhoeffer said this of the Nazis and Hitler. In a banned radio broadcast in 1933, he declared:

If a leader allows himself to be persuaded by those he leads who want to turn him into an idol...then the image of the leader will degenerate into a misleader. The leader who makes an idol of himself and his office makes a mockery of God.

Christians who believe religion and politics should be separate

Some Christians feel religion and politics do not go together. They argue that non-Christians resent religious involvement in secular matters and that a Christian should be concerned about spiritual development rather than politics. They claim that Christian teaching is concerned with loving God and other people, but society is run on a secular, not a religious, basis and it should depend on political, not Christian, principles. Moreover, British society is multi-cultural and made up of a number of religious faiths and it may be that, to avoid conflict, all religions should stay out of politics. When religious leaders, such as the pope or the archbishop of Canterbury, make statements on political matters, they are often criticised for interfering in matters that, some say, are none of their business.

There is some support for this view in the Bible. Jesus approved the payment of taxes to the Roman government, which occupied Israel during his lifetime (Luke 20:20–26), but he did not suggest it was a religious issue or that it impeded religious observance and obedience to God. Furthermore, he avoided being drawn into situations that would have made him seem to offer a direct threat to the political system at the time: 'When Jesus realised that they were about to come and take him by force and make him king, he withdrew again to the mountain by himself' (John 6:15).

Elsewhere in the Bible, St Paul tells the early Christians that they should obey political leaders because authority has been given to them by God. In other words, God is in charge of the politics of the world and Christians should accept their political leaders.

Everyone must submit himself to the governing authorities, for there is no authority except that which God has established. The authorities that exist have been established by God.

(Romans 13:1)

> Remind the people to be subject to rulers and authorities, to be obedient, to be ready to do whatever is good.
>
> (Titus 3:1)

For many Christians, therefore, the challenge is to obey the government when it seems to be promoting non-Christian principles and to offer a Christian view on politics. With this in mind, some Churches may offer support to the government in the process of changing the law.

> The law must constantly be checked and updated for fairness. Respect for the law may require that particular laws are contested and reformed.
>
> (*Accept and Resist,* Methodist conference report, 1986)

The Welfare State

The **Welfare State** is the name given to the system set up by the government to try to help the poorest groups in society — the unemployed, the sick, the disabled and the elderly. The Church has always been involved in work to help the poor and needy. The Welfare State was started when Christians like Lord Shaftesbury, William Wilberforce and others campaigned against poverty in Britain in the nineteenth century.

Poverty was widespread in nineteenth-century Britain

Concern for the conditions of the poor and needy is often associated with utilitarianism — a political and ethical way of addressing the needs of the majority. The utilitarian principle of aiming to bring about the greatest happiness for the greatest number of people influenced many important social and political movements in the nineteenth century, including prison reform, Dr Barnardo's homes for homeless children, and even the development of the postal service. Not all Christians agree that utilitarianism is a good ethic. They argue that happiness is not the most important goal for humans, compared with, say, compassion and

Key word

Welfare State
A system whereby the government ensures that the basic needs of the poorest members of society are met

obedience to God's law. However, utilitarianism does aim to achieve a fair state for everyone, and so it indirectly reflects some important Christian values.

In the nineteenth century there was little state provision, but by the turn of the twentieth century old-age pensions had been introduced. During the Second World War, a committee was set up by the government to look at social issues and the result was the Beveridge Report of 1942, which highlighted five areas of concern in Britain:

- Want: a large number of people lived in poverty because they were sick, unemployed or widows.
- Disease: there was no free medical treatment and the poorest people could not afford to see a doctor.
- Ignorance: free secondary education was only for those who won a scholarship. Most children left school at 14 with only a basic education.
- Squalor: many people were living in slums.
- Idleness: nearly 10% of the workforce was unemployed at the start of the Second World War.

As a result, successive governments introduced ways of relieving poverty and suffering, and the Welfare State came into being. The new measures included:

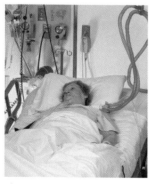

The NHS provides free healthcare for all

- Secondary schools were made free for everyone and the school leaving age was raised to 15.
- National insurance and financial benefits were introduced to help the unemployed.
- The National Health Service (NHS) was set up to establish free healthcare for all.
- Thousands of new council houses were built and slums were demolished.
- Nationalised industries and employment boards were set up to provide work for the unemployed.

Arguments in favour of the Welfare State

- The Welfare State ensures that everyone gets treated equally in education, health and housing.

- It avoids the unfairness of the rich getting better treatment than the poor.
- The Welfare State ensures that nobody suffers extreme hardship and poverty.
- It is based on Christian principles of loving and caring for others.

Arguments against the Welfare State

- It is expensive to run.
- As new, more expensive, medical treatments are developed, the NHS has to spend yet more money.
- Social security benefits may make some people reluctant to get a job.
- The private sector provides better services than the public sector.
- Pensions are particularly expensive.

The Welfare State in the twenty-first century

Adults in work pay taxes and national insurance to provide the services of the Welfare State. The Welfare State gives:
- free secondary education for everyone up to the age of 18 and financial help for poorer students at university
- free hospital care and some NHS provision for dental and optical costs; payments are also made to people who are too ill to go to work
- payments and benefits to the unemployed
- old-age pensions
- child benefit for children at school
- housing benefit for those eligible
- the unemployed help at job centres so they can find work

The Christian basis of the Welfare State

The Welfare State is based on Christian principles contained in the Bible in the Ten Commandments and the Sermon on the Mount. The Ten Commandments (Decalogue) in Exodus 20:1–20 highlight the importance of respecting and helping other people. For example:
- Honour your parents — for instance, look after the elderly.
- Do not murder — this could include making sure there is healthcare available to prevent people dying from illness unnecessarily.

- Do not steal — this includes helping the poor and needy.
- Do not commit adultery.
- Do not give false evidence.
- Do not covet other people's belongings.

The Golden Rule, a mosaic by Norman Rockwell

Key word

Golden Rule
Jesus's teaching that people should treat other people in the same way they themselves would like to be treated

Above all, Jesus gave what many Christians call the **Golden Rule**. This is a guide to the way in which people must treat others. It teaches that all Christians, rich and poor, should ensure everyone is properly cared for: 'Do to others what you would have them do to you' (Matthew 7:12).

Christians are frequently involved, therefore, in establishing social systems that are important for everyone: educating children, helping the sick and caring for the homeless. Jesus's teaching on welfare is best illustrated in the parable of the sheep and goats (Matthew 25:31–46). Jesus taught that it is a Christian duty to feed those who are hungry, give clothes to the naked, give water to the thirsty, visit the sick and help those who are in prison. If Christians do these things for people in need, they are doing them for Jesus:

'Lord, when did we see you hungry and feed you, or thirsty and give you something to drink? When did we see you a stranger and invite you in or needing clothes and clothe you? When did we see you sick or in prison and go to visit you?' The King will reply, 'I tell you the truth, whatever you did for one of the least of these brothers of mine, you did for me.'

(Matthew 25:37–40)

In the same way, Jesus spoke of the need for good deeds and actions to go alongside a person's faith in God. To have faith by itself is not enough — faith without works is of little use and the believer who does not do good works will see his faith fade away.

You foolish man, do you want evidence that faith without deeds is useless?… As the body without the spirit is dead, so faith without deeds is dead.

(James 2:20,26)

Questions and activities

Sample questions and answers

1 Give two of the Ten Commandments. (2 marks)

'You shall not commit adultery' (20:14) and 'You shall not covet your neighbour's house' (20:17).

2 Outline the ways in which a Christian might make a moral decision. (6 marks)

Christians may make a moral decision by following the teachings in the Bible. The Ten Commandments contain a number of guidelines to help with a range of moral issues, including respect for other people, family matters, possessions and criminal actions. The Bible also contains the teachings of Jesus, and the Sermon on the Mount teaches about the importance of treating others fairly and with love and respect: 'Love your enemies and pray for those who persecute you' (Matthew 5:44).

The parable of the sheep and goats reminds Christians that when they help others they are doing God's work and the Golden Rule speaks of the importance of treating others as we would like to be treated.

Christians may also make moral decisions with the help of the teachings of the Christian Church. In their local church, they might talk to the priest and ask for his or her guidance. Alternatively, they could look at the teachings of the Church, contained in encyclicals, catechisms and other pronouncements from the pope or the Synod. These give guidance on a large number of modern dilemmas, including abortion and homosexuality.

3 Explain the relationship between the teachings of the Bible and the work of the Welfare State. (8 marks)

The Welfare State is based on the need to care for the less fortunate members of society. There is a clear relationship between the provisions of the Welfare State and the teachings of the Bible. For instance, the Ten Commandments (Exodus 20) highlight the importance of helping other people and the commandment 'Honour your father and your mother' (20:12) means that people should ensure that the elderly are properly looked after. In the same way, 'You shall not murder' (20:13) could be said to include making sure that there is proper healthcare for everyone, so that nobody dies unnecessarily. Meanwhile, 'You shall not steal' (20:15) is a reminder to help the poor and needy and this could include not exploiting them but instead providing shelter and money.

Similarly, when Jesus gave the Golden Rule that people should treat one another as they would like to be treated themselves, he was saying that the priority of a society should be to ensure that everyone has equal access to the basics of life — food, shelter, education and healthcare. In the parable of the sheep and goats, Jesus said that when people help those in need, they are doing God's work.

The Welfare State tries to fulfil these teachings. It provides money and shelter for the poor, hospitals for the sick, free education for all children and healthcare for everyone. It may not be a perfect system, but it is a genuine attempt to fulfil the teachings of the Bible in a modern society.

4 'Christians should keep out of politics.' Do you agree? Give reasons for your opinion, showing you have considered another point of view. In your answer, you should refer to Christianity.

(4 marks)

There are several reasons why some may argue that Christians should keep out of politics. The UK is a secular society and therefore politics should be run on a secular pattern. The majority of people are not deeply religious and do not necessarily agree with Christian moral principles. The UK is also a multi-faith society and it would be wrong for the political system to favour Christian moral views over those of other faiths. A Christian should be concerned with spiritual matters rather than political ones.

However, there are good reasons why Christians should be involved in politics, and indeed many MPs and other political figures are Christians. Jesus was involved in politics and taught about the need to pay taxes and obey the authorities, and he also challenged the authorities when he thought they were wrong. A Christian who

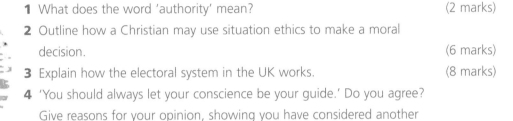

is involved in politics can try to apply Jesus's teaching to help to provide for the poor and needy in society, just as famous Christians such as Lord Shaftesbury did in the past.

In principle, therefore, it seems wise for Christians to be aware of what is happening within politics and to be involved when they can make a special contribution, but to recognise that politics is for people of all faiths and for those without faith, all of whom should be allowed to be equally involved.

Further questions

1 What does the word 'authority' mean? (2 marks)

2 Outline how a Christian may use situation ethics to make a moral decision. (6 marks)

3 Explain how the electoral system in the UK works. (8 marks)

4 'You should always let your conscience be your guide.' Do you agree? Give reasons for your opinion, showing you have considered another point of view. In your answer, you should refer to Christianity. (4 marks)

Class activities and homework

Understanding authority

In pairs or small groups, draw a circle in the middle of a large sheet of paper and write 'Christian authority' inside it. Using coloured pens, draw a spider diagram from the centre outwards, highlighting the different types of authority that may influence a Christian and how they would do so, for example the Bible, the Church. Your teacher will then pose a dilemma: for example, should a Christian have pre-marital sex? Brainstorm the advice each source of authority would give in answer to the dilemma and add your solutions to the diagram. Under your teacher's guidance, share your views with the rest of the class.

'The Bible was written thousands of years ago and cannot possibly offer good moral advice to Christians today.' Do you agree? Give reasons for your opinion, showing you have considered other points of view.

Understanding moral dilemmas

Your teacher will divide your class into three groups, and give each group one of the three dilemmas outlined below.

1 Parents are told their unborn child is severely disabled. Should they have an abortion?

2 A twice-divorced person wants to get married in a church.

3 A terminally ill patient will die in a few days' time. Should a doctor give a pain-killing injection, which she knows will end the person's life earlier?

In relation to the dilemma you have been given, answer the following three questions:

1 How would a Christian respond?

2 How would you or one of your friends respond?

3 How would your parents respond?

Under your teacher's guidance, share your views with the rest of the class.

If a Christian won £5 million on the lottery, how should they spend the money? Give reasons for your answer.

Understanding elections

Your teacher will guide you in holding a class general election for a parliament with 500 seats. Choose six people to stand for election, including at least one from each of the mainstream political parties. Each will speak for 1 minute on their policies. After they have all spoken, cast your votes. Write '1' next to the name of your favourite candidate, '2' next to the name of your second favourite, and so on down to '6' for your least favourite.

Count the votes in two ways. First see which party wins in a first-past-the-post result in which only the number 1 vote is counted. This party wins all 500 seats. Then see how many seats each party would win under proportional representation, where it is the percentage of the vote that counts. What is the difference between the two results? Discuss which system is the best and why.

What are the advantages and disadvantages of living in a democratic country?

Understanding national and local government

In pairs or small groups, look at a newspaper. Find as many articles as you can that are concerned with (a) national government and (b) local government. In your group, decide on the three most important issues that you think are facing the national government today and the local government in your area. How do you think these issues should be solved? Under your teacher's guidance, share your views with the rest of the class.

'Religion should be kept out of politics.' Do you agree? Give reasons for your opinion, showing you have considered other points of view.

Understanding the Welfare State

In pairs, research how the Welfare State is involved in your local area in (a) education, (b) health, (c) the elderly and (d) the unemployed. Under your teacher's guidance, share your views with the rest of the class and consider whether or not the provision is enough and, if not, what more you think could be done.

What are the arguments for and against the Welfare State? Is the Welfare State a good or a bad thing and is there a better alternative?

Section 2

Religion and the environment

Pollution

Pollution is the contamination of the environment. Pollution damages and spoils the environment so that it is no longer clean, healthy and able to provide the best possible conditions for humans, animals and plants. There are many forms of pollution, although it is only recently that people have become concerned

Key word

Pollution
The contamination of the natural environment

about it. During the Industrial Revolution, when factories and manufacturing industries were developing rapidly, the advantages of these developments were more important than investigating the possible damage they could cause. The extent of the damage caused by industrial pollution was not known or measured until many years later. Today, individuals, communities, governments and organisations are concerned about the pollution of the environment. Nothing on the earth works on its own — everything is involved in an ecosystem in which everything depends on everything else. Animals, plants and humans are all part of a cycle that depends on and affects the environment. If one element of that cycle changes, everything else in the cycle is eventually affected too.

Causes of pollution

Pollution is caused by people and the way they make use of the environment and its resources.

Increased technology constantly leads to the development of new products. People want these products, but the manufacture of them often causes pollution. The more products people buy, the more they throw away, and one of the biggest environmental concerns is waste. Most domestic waste cannot be recycled, and is not biodegradable — it does not break down naturally if buried or exposed. Just think what happens to all those mobile phones and computers people constantly replace. They cannot give them away to other people because everyone wants to upgrade. Some are sent to developing countries, but many are just dumped. Waste takes up space, spreads disease and releases dangerous chemicals into the environment, but people are producing more waste, not less, every year.

The population of the earth is increasing and is likely to rise to close to 10 billion within your lifetime. All these people make demands on the environment, either in terms of what they take from it or what they release into it.

People are lazy about caring for the environment. One of the biggest pollutants in the world is cars, and yet people often use the car when they could walk. Public transport can carry hundreds more people on a single journey than a car, but many people do not like to use it, and if it is not well run only those with no other option make use of it. Few people recycle products, even when provision is made to do so. Clothes, household goods, books and furniture can all be recycled, but some people are not prepared to buy or exchange second-hand goods.

Air pollution

Land pollution

Water pollution

Noise pollution

There are four main types of pollution:

- Air pollution: smoke from industry and sometimes homes pollutes the atmosphere and can cause breathing illnesses such as asthma.
- Land pollution: land is damaged by dumping household or industrial waste. This spreads disease, which affects wildlife, humans and crops.
- Water pollution: waste dumped at sea — usually sewage, oil or chemicals — affects land, rivers, animals, birds and humans. There are huge penalties payable by industries that cause water pollution. Despite these penalties, there are often reports of oil spillages that kill thousands of sea birds and animals.
- Noise pollution: this may seem a less obvious form of pollution, but loud and persistent noise causes great distress. People can suffer hearing damage from industrial noise, and emotional trauma from loud music, traffic or aircraft. Properties near bypasses or airports often go down in value, so people who bought them before the road or airport was built, or when it was less busy, lose money.

All these forms of pollution can affect any country in the world. Even if a country has not been responsible for pollution, it can be affected by poor pollution controls in other countries. The only way to decrease pollution is if all the nations of the world agree to limit it. Developed nations, such as the UK, have strict anti-pollution laws, but it is harder to enforce these on less economically developed countries (LEDCs), which are still trying to build and develop their industries.

Effects of pollution

The effects of years of increasing pollution are now becoming clear. One of the major and most worrying effects is **global warming**. This is caused by the carbon dioxide released when coal and oil are burnt to generate electricity. Carbon dioxide in the atmosphere acts rather like the glass of a greenhouse — it allows the sun's energy in but does not allow heat to get out. To some extent this is natural and makes the earth warm enough for us to live on, but increased levels of carbon dioxide are causing climate change known as global warming. The environmental effects of this increased warmth are already evident in melting polar regions. Wildlife is directly affected, and penguins, polar bears, seals and their natural food supplies are suffering. Global warming affects other areas too, even the UK. It is thought that the temperature will rise over the next 50 years and that this will cause problems such as desertification and flooding all over the world.

Trees take in carbon dioxide and release oxygen, which humans depend on for survival. However, because vast areas of tropical rainforest are being destroyed, there are fewer trees to deal with increasing levels of carbon dioxide. This deforestation means that the soil in which the trees grew disappears and the land becomes desertified (like a desert). The reasons for deforestation are highly controversial. Global companies, such as McDonald's, are thought by some to be guilty of an irresponsible attitude to the environment, encouraging the destruction of forest and prairie areas to increase cattle grazing, which ultimately leads to the production of unhealthy fast-food products.

Large areas of tropical rainforest are being destroyed

Key word

Global warming
Increased carbon dioxide in the atmosphere raises the temperature of the earth, with potentially devastating effects on the environment

Three other forms of pollution affect the environment:

- **Acid rain**: acid is formed in the air from sulphur dioxide and nitrogen oxide, which are emitted by power stations, industry and motor vehicles. These gases form acids when they mix with water (sulphuric acid and nitric acid), which fall to earth in rain. Acid rain may cause damage to buildings and vegetation. It can be carried by the wind across seas and national boundaries. For example, Swedish forests have been affected by burning fossil fuels in the UK.

- Radioactive pollution: although nuclear power stations do not produce carbon dioxide or acid rain, they do produce nuclear waste, which is extremely dangerous to humans and animals. Accidents in nuclear plants create damage that can take thousands of years to repair and spreads hundreds of kilometres.

- Eutrophication: fertilisers and sewage disposal release large quantities of nitrogen into rivers and streams. This encourages the rapid growth of plants. When these plants die the bacteria which feed on them use oxygen from the water. This causes fish to suffocate because they cannot get enough oxygen from the water, so polluting the water supplies themselves.

> **Key word**
>
> **Acid rain**
> Burning fossil fuels generates sulphuric acid and nitric acid, which make rain more acidic. This affects vegetation and buildings

The problems of natural resources

Natural resources are provided by nature and can be divided into two types: **non-renewable** and **renewable resources**.

Non-renewable resources

Coal, gas and oil are non-renewable resources. They cannot be replaced once they have been taken from the environment. Not only are they used to run vehicles on the land, in the air and at sea, they are also used to provide electricity, a product that is often wasted. Leaving lights, computers or the television switched on (even in standby mode) all needlessly uses electricity that cannot be replaced. It is not just a question of higher electricity bills for the householder, but a resource that everyone needs has been wasted.

Other products made from non-renewable resources that are often wasted are metal and plastic. Recycling is essential if manufacturers are to cut down on these products and save more electricity for running essential services such as hospitals and emergency services.

Renewable resources

One way of saving valuable non-renewable resources is to use renewable resources where they can perform the same function. Renewable resources replace themselves after they have been used. They include wind power, solar (sun) power, wave power and water power, as well as products such as sugar cane which can be used in place of petrol. Nuclear power is also renewable, but because of its potential dangers it is less attractive as an alternative. Wind power can only be used in some climatic conditions and it relies on turbines, which are not attractive in the landscape. Wave power is a renewable energy source, but it is expensive. Solar power is already a popular alternative energy source, and can be used for heating, lighting and powering computers and other hardware that traditionally runs from electricity or battery power.

Although wider use of renewable resources must be developed, it is a slow process as it requires people to accept changes in lifestyle. Industries are often slow to change methods of production that may affect their profits, even in the long-term interests of the environment. Traditional energy providers such as oil, petrol, gas and electricity companies also have a vested interest in slowing the rate of development of renewable energy sources. It has been suggested that cars could run on solar power even now had the petrol companies not ensured that they were not developed for this purpose. As it is, alternative sources of energy are often presented as odd and of short-term value.

A wind turbine

Key words

Natural resources
Natural products and environments that are used by humans — coal, oil, fertile land and gas, for example

Non-renewable resources
Natural resources which cannot be replaced, such as coal

Renewable resources
Natural resources which can be renewed by replanting, such as trees, or which replenish themselves, such as sunshine

Food resources

In many parts of the world starvation causes disease and death. The reasons are sometimes climatic — drought and crop spoilage — and sometimes because of war or because a country cannot afford to buy food from other countries. A country may grow cash crops (fast-growing crops such as cotton), which it exports, but such crops do not feed its own population. Often land is reused to grow crops with little success, or the land is turned over for grazing, so it loses any value it may have had to grow crops.

There is increasing concern about how people in the more economically developed world choose unhealthy foods while less economically developed countries are still struggling to provide a basic diet for many of their inhabitants. In the West, considerable resources are used to produce fast foods, confectionery, snacks and fizzy drinks, leading to obesity and poor health. Farmers and producers in LEDCs often provide basic resources to Western manufacturers but get very little in return.

Protecting the environment

Planting trees helps to conserve the environment

Although many individuals, politicians and industries are slow to act on environmental concerns, the environment has become an increasingly political and social issue over the last 30 years. In 1997, 55 countries signed the Kyoto Agreement, making a commitment to cut the amount of greenhouse gases they produce by 5.2% a year. However, the USA — the biggest producer of greenhouse gases, with cheap and plentiful petrol — refused to sign the agreement. The USA opted instead to increase forest size to produce the same effect. There is also an increasing move towards investing in the development and use of renewable resources and local and national initiatives to encourage recycling. Already there have been some changes. For example, cars now produce less pollution than they did 30 years ago and this will become even lower over the next 5 years. Many people are actively adopting more environmentally friendly lifestyles, such as cycling rather than driving, installing more energy-efficient household appliances, and buying foodstuffs from organic or fair-trade suppliers.

Religious attitudes to protecting the environment

As long ago as 1986, representatives of **conservation** agencies and world religions met to discuss environmental concerns. Each organisation produced a statement of belief in response to their discussions. Christian representatives declared: 'Christians repudiate all ill-considered exploitation of nature which threatens to destroy it and, in turn, to make man the victim of degradation.' Muslim representatives observed: 'Allah's trustees [all Muslims] are responsible for maintaining the unity of his creation, the integrity of the earth, its flora and fauna, its wildlife and its natural environment.'

Christian views

> Although God put humans in charge of the resources of the universe, this power must be used with concern for the rights of neighbours and future generations.
>
> (Catechism of the Catholic Church)

At the heart of the Christian attitude to the environment is the concept of **stewardship**. This is the view that the earth was created by God and given to human beings to care for and protect. Stewardship is a duty that involves responsibility. This teaching is clearly set out in the **creation** story in Genesis: 'God blessed them, and said to them, "Be fruitful and multiply. Rule over the fish of the sea and the birds of the air and over every living thing that moves on the ground"' (Genesis 1:28). This means that God gave humanity what is called dominion (authority) over creation. However, that authority is to be used wisely and compassionately. God also gave humanity the responsibility to 'till the earth and keep it' (Genesis 2:15). This clearly suggests that the earth will not look after itself. Humanity must look after it on behalf of God.

Key words

Conservation
Preserving and protecting the environment and its natural resources

Creation
God making the earth out of nothing

Stewardship
Taking care of the environment on behalf of God and for the benefit of future generations

Adam and Eve in Paradise by Jan Brueghel and P. P. Rubens

> When I consider your heavens, the work of your fingers…what is man that you are mindful of him? You made him a little lower than the heavenly beings…. You made him rule over the work of your hands; you put everything under his feet.
>
> (Psalm 8.3–6)

Interestingly, it was only after the Fall — when man and woman disobeyed God in the Garden of Eden — that the task of keeping the land became a struggle. God told Adam: 'Cursed is the ground because of you; in toil you shall eat of it all the days of your life; thorns and thistles it shall bring forth for you; and you will eat the plants of the field' (Genesis 3:17–18). Clearly, after the Fall, humans were not going to find stewardship easy or fulfilling. Creation had originally been perfectly good, and would have provided everything that humans needed to live well, but now it would become a challenge.

Christians believe that they are called to change the effects of the Fall where they can. Although perfection cannot be achieved fully until heaven, the parable of the talents suggests that Christians should leave the earth in a better condition than that in which they found it.

> I tell you, to all those who have, more will be given; but from those who have nothing, even what they have will be taken away.
>
> (Luke 19:26)

It is obvious that polluting the planet is not responsible stewardship, and draining natural resources is not only selfish and greedy but abuses the gifts God gave in creation. Furthermore, it does not show love to a neighbour, either in the present or in future generations. Christians believe the earth belongs to God and is held in trust for future generations, so it can never be said to belong to anyone. Thus, Christians have a responsibility to work towards reducing pollution and cutting back on the use of non-renewable resources, to share natural resources more fairly, and to support environmental groups.

However, in some respects, Christians exercise caution in these areas. Some non-Christian groups which adopt a 'new age' approach to the environment carry out environmental work and see the earth and its resources as something to be honoured, even worshipped, apart from God. Christians emphasise that, while the environment is a gift from God, it is not holy in itself and humans are not called to worship it. Only God the creator is worthy of worship. Humans should not seek to become at one with the environment or to be subject to it. People are at the climax of God's creation, and so although conservation of the environment is of vital concern, it should not be at the expense of people. For example, if hundreds of people were going to be made homeless and unemployed by putting an environmentally unfriendly company out of business, Christians would put the needs of the employees first, before conserving the environment.

Some environmentalists approach their work in a way that many Christians find questionable, and it is important for Christians to know that the environmental groups they support are motivated by a genuine concern for the planet and are not pursuing a radical political or social agenda.

Islamic views

The sun and moon follow courses exactly computed; And the herbs and the trees — both alike bow in adoration. And the firmament he has raised high, and he has set up the balance in order that you may not transgress that balance.

(Surah 55:5–8)

There is no altering the laws of Allah's creation.

(Surah 30:30)

Key word

Khalifah
The Islamic
principle that
humans have a
responsibility to
act as Allah's
representatives
on earth

Islam too teaches that Muslims have been placed in a position of responsibility over the earth and its resources and have a duty to care for it according to Allah's principles. Although human needs take priority, the principle of Tawhid means there is a unity in creation that must be respected. The whole universe — humans, animals and the environment — is in balance and Allah made humans as his **Khalifah** (rulers for him) to look after the earth. One of the things on which humans will be judged on the Day of Judgement is how well they have carried out this responsibility.

Islam also teaches that Adam was made a ruler over creation, to whom even the angels were subject: 'It is he who has made you custodians, inheritors of the earth' (Surah 6:165). The workings of nature, however, remain subject to Allah's will and reveal his nature and purpose to humans.

> Behold in the creation of the heavens and the earth; in the alteration of the night and the day…in the rain which God sends down from the skies, and the life which he gives therewith…in the beasts of all kinds that he scatters through the earth; in the change of the wind and the clouds…here indeed are signs for a people that are wise.
>
> (Surah 2:164)

Those who do not accept this divinely ordered state of affairs are like Iblis (Satan) who 'was of those who reject the faith' (Surah 2:34).

Muslims should be aware of how they affect the environment positively and negatively — avoiding waste and pollution, using recycled and bio-degradable products and reducing energy use. Planting trees and crops, taking care of them, and using them for the good of others will be blessed by Allah.

The work of religious organisations in conserving the environment

The National Religious Partnership for the Environment (NRPE)

The NRPE was founded in 1993 by four major US religious organisations and alliances:

- The US Catholic Conference (USCC): the policy agencies for all bishops, clergy and parishes of the Catholic Church in the USA.
- The National Council of Churches of Christ (NCCC): a group of 34 Protestant, Eastern Orthodox and African–American denominations.
- The Coalition on Environment and Jewish Life (COEJL): an alliance of agencies and organisations across all four Jewish movements.
- The Evangelical Environmental Network (EEN): a group of 23 Evangelical Christian programme and educational institutions.

The partnership seeks to care for God's creation throughout religious life and to provide inspiration, moral vision and commitment to social justice to protect the environment and humans within it. It draws on religious teachings and traditions, as well as science and economics. It encourages efforts across racial, ethnic, gender, economic, political and cultural boundaries. The partnership works with public policy agencies and networks to discuss the environment and visits schools, colleges and religious groups.

> Created in the very image of God, human beings have a unique relationship to the Creator; at the same time we are creatures, shaped by the same processes and embedded in the same systems of physical, chemical and biological interconnections which sustain other creatures. Called to be the Creator's special stewards, human beings have a unique responsibility for the rest of creation. As wise stewards, we are summoned not only to mould creation's bounty into complex civilisations of justice and beauty, but also to sustain creation's fruitfulness and preserve its powerful testimony to its Creator. We confess that too often we have perverted our stewardly calling, rampaging destructively through creation rather than offering creation and civilisation back in praise to the Creator. For this our sin, we repent, gratefully acknowledging that the Creator is also the Redeemer who promises to renew all things. In grateful obedience to this our marvellous God, we resolve to make our homes, our faith communities and our societies centres for creation's care and renewal, healing the damaged fabric of the creation which God entrusted to us.
>
> (NRPE website)

Other religious organisations that work for the environment

A conservation project in Ethiopia funded by Christian Aid

Muslim Aid works to conserve the environment in threatened places such as Afghanistan, while Christian Aid works worldwide to protect the environment and encourage development. Target Earth provides opportunities for Christians to work to conserve the earth and the Eden Conservancy, established in 1993 to remedy problems caused by cutting down forests, buys endangered land. The Jewish National Fund works specifically in Israel to remove pollution and conserve natural resources and to make dumps, landfill sites and quarries safe. It has planted 200 million trees to absorb carbon dioxide and reduce desertification. It has also developed ways to make the desert more productive for farming.

Animal rights

Do animals have rights?

The role of animals is often a difficult one for religious believers because they have to find a balance between recognising animals as fellow creatures made by and loved by God, and maintaining the order of creation in which humans were placed above the rest of creation. It is thought that animals can be used in some ways for the benefit of humans, but that they should also be respected. How far that respect should extend is an important question. For some people, it means refusing to eat or use any animal products, and giving to animals exactly the same respect that would be extended to humans — sometimes more. For others, it means making use of the food and products that animals provide, but doing so in a humane manner.

Key word

Animal rights
The principle that animals have the right not to be exploited by human beings

If animals have rights, it means humans also have responsibilities to protect those rights. Arguments given in favour of **animal rights** include the fact that many humans who are not able to express their rights or act on them still have rights — children, elderly people, mentally disabled or terminally ill people, for example. Their rights are claimed and protected by other people who act on their behalf. Even the rights of an unborn foetus can be represented by someone acting in its interest. Therefore, having rights cannot simply be a matter of being able to express them and, on these grounds alone, animals could be said to have rights. In the nineteenth century, the philosopher and politician Jeremy Bentham believed that the time would come when animals would be thought to have rights simply on the basis that they could feel pain. This was a radical view for his time, but it is morally and philosophically reasonable. Humans believe they have the right to be protected from pain because they know how it feels and that it is natural to avoid it. Why should the case not be the same for animals? In the twentieth century, the American philosopher Peter Singer used the term 'speciesism' to describe the attitude that humans are superior to animals, comparing it to racism and suggesting it is just as wrong.

Humans believe they should be recognised as having value in themselves. If animals have rights, this must include the right to be recognised in the same way.

However, some people argue that animals do not have rights because they cannot claim those rights and protect them. Only those who can make a choice can have rights, and since animals do not have choices in the moral sense of the term, they cannot have rights. Another argument is that while humans have reason — the ability to think, plan, look ahead, make judgements and assess the consequences of their actions — animals do not. They act on instinct. Animals cannot communicate and think in the same way humans do, and it may be argued, therefore, that it is not enough to say that animals have rights because they can feel pain.

Human societies go beyond the need to survive, but animal societies are essentially based on the survival of the fittest. Humans seem to be capable of seeking a relationship with God and questioning their destiny beyond death. The crucial stage of human development — when humans developed a frontal lobe that enabled them to think about the future — coincided with the development of a religious sense that enabled them to find hope and purpose in the midst of death and suffering. There is no evidence that animals have this sense.

Animal experimentation

One of the biggest areas of concern for those who seek to protect the rights of animals is the use of animals in experimentation. The development of many products has been made possible by testing them on animals. Items tested include cosmetics, toiletries, medicines and vaccines, household

products like bleach and washing-up liquid, food additives and weaponry, particularly biological and chemical weapons. It is assumed that if these products are safe for dogs, chimpanzees and rabbits, they will be safe for humans. Because of the level of feeling against animal experimentation in the late-twentieth century, most animal testing is now carried out on mice and rats bred for the purpose.

Animal rights activists protest against experiments on animals

Obviously, there are many ethical questions raised about making use of animals in this way. Are the products essential? There are so many cosmetics and toiletries on the market, does the development of more justify the use of animals? 'Beauty without cruelty' is now considered to be an important market label for most manufacturers of beauty products, who specify that their products are developed without animal testing. A leader in this field is The Body Shop, which built its reputation in the early 1980s as the first high-street cosmetics retailer to deliver guaranteed cruelty-free and fair-trade beauty products.

The manufacture of household and industrial cleaning and maintenance products must also now be possible without using animal testing, but the development of new medications and vaccines raises different questions. Without animal testing, it is unlikely, if not impossible, that researchers into cures for cancer, multiple sclerosis, heart disease, cystic fibrosis, AIDS/HIV and many other fatal illnesses would have been able to save the lives of millions of people worldwide. The argument in favour of experimentation on animals to develop drugs rests on the belief that human health is more important than animal welfare. Testing drugs in the early stages of their development on humans could be fatal and few people would volunteer. By using animals, humans need not be brought in until much later in the process when the safety of the drug has been established. Insulin — a vital means of controlling some forms of diabetes — was not only tested on animals but is obtained from them.

This view is a utilitarian view, based on the argument that if a considerable number of people are to benefit from animal testing, it is justified by the long-term consequences. However, there are strong arguments against this view. It is possible to argue that drug development that requires animal experimentation simply should not be done — the ends cannot justify the means. It could be argued that drugs are only needed to cure illnesses because not enough is done to prevent them. Better education in healthy eating and lifestyle and better treatment of patients in the early stages of diseases before they become fatal could prevent many of the illnesses for which drugs are being developed. Furthermore, new technology has created possibilities for testing that do not use animals: cell culture, *in vitro* research and computer research, for example.

Thalidomide

In the early 1960s, many pregnant women were prescribed a new drug, Thalidomide, to prevent morning sickness. Although the drug had been tested on animals, none of the animals had been pregnant. Many women subsequently gave birth to babies with severe abnormalities. If the drug had been tested on pregnant animals, this might have been prevented.

Using animals for food

If animal experimentation is wrong because it involves cruelty to animals, killing animals for food may be considered just as wrong. Around 10% of people in the UK are vegetarians, many of whom choose not to eat meat on moral grounds. They argue that because meat is not essential in the human diet, there is no justification for killing animals to provide needless luxury foodstuffs. Vegans take the argument further. They refuse to eat any food products (including dairy foods) that come from animals on the grounds that the production of these foods still involves cruelty and animal exploitation. Nevertheless, most people eat meat or animal products at some point in their lives, and those who do so as a matter of course argue that there is a big difference between animal experimentation and eating meat.

The arguments against eating meat are strong. Even though humans have canine teeth, they can live healthily — perhaps even more healthily — without eating meat. There is also a strong argument that the conditions in which farm animals and birds are kept are morally wrong. Hens are often kept in battery cages that give them little, if any, room to move. Some cattle  and pigs are also kept indoors and fed artificial food stuffs which make them more commercially valuable. Some animals are reared to provide luxury meats or meat products, which involve them living in particularly shocking conditions, being kept in the dark and force-fed over a very short life span, for example.

Some pigs are kept indoors in small pens

Organically-reared meat comes from animals which live free range and have had a reasonably good quality of life and diet before they are killed. However, it is more expensive to rear animals in this way, and both the farmer and the consumer bear the cost. Not all are willing to do so and, ultimately, these animals still have to be killed.

Even if large numbers of people adopted vegetarianism as a way of life, farmers' interests and the interests of animals they were already rearing would have to be taken into account. Already many farmers struggle to survive, and to force them all into organic or free-range farming, or to forbid rearing meat for food altogether, would have devastating consequences for the economy.

Other uses for animals

Animals can be used to help humans in ways that do not involve their suffering and death. Guide dogs have been used by blind people for many years, but today the value of animals in helping humans is recognised to stretch much further. Dogs can be trained to help the disabled, the deaf and the chronically ill, and the value of pets is thought to be considerable. Pets as Therapy is an organisation that takes pets into hospitals, nursing homes and homes for the elderly. Patients gain tremendous comfort from touching and stroking animals, and it has been suggested that having a pet can add several years to a person's lifespan.

Animals have traditionally been of enormous help to humans in farming and industry, in ways that have not necessarily cost them their lives. However, many uses of animals are now strictly controlled: for example bull fights, beach donkeys, and animals in circuses and zoos. There is a fine line between partnership with animals in trade, tourism and industry, and the exploitation of animals that cannot speak for themselves.

Blood sports

Hunting used to be a necessary part of human survival and being a good hunter would often lead to someone becoming head of their tribe. Animals provided food, clothing, fuel and weapons, so hunting was a way of life. In some parts of the world, it is still necessary to hunt to feed the family or tribe, but in the UK hunting is a sport that gives rise to great controversy. Those who support it claim it is an important part of conservation that helps to kill weak and elderly animals and keep their populations down, as well as protecting livestock from foxes and other predators.

However, opponents of hunting question the humanity of the sport, which often involves chasing a fox until it is too tired to run any further and is torn apart by hunting dogs. Even shooting deer can be barbaric if the animal is not killed instantly. The fact that these sports are called 'blood sports' is not a coincidence.

Shooting game birds is limited to certain seasons, but using beaters to make birds fly into the air to be shot at is considered by many to be cruel. However, the birds are allowed to live freely before being shot and, in this sense at least, they are better off than battery hens, for example. Some claim that fishing is cruel even if the fish are returned to the water after being caught. While anglers maintain that fish cannot remember the experience, opponents disagree and argue that fishing is a blood sport like any other.

Clothing

Breeding or hunting animals for their fur is largely considered wrong today and few people wear real fur in public. Leather is less of an issue because it is a by-product of animals that have already been killed for food, although vegetarians or vegans may refuse to use leather bags or wear leather shoes or belts.

Religious attitudes to animals and their use

Christian views

Christians believe animals are part of God's creation, and so are subject to the same principles of stewardship that apply to the rest of the natural world. Humans were put in charge of animals at creation, and so are responsible

Free-range hens have a better life than those kept in cages

Key word

Sin
An act against the will of God

for their care. Humane and compassionate treatment of animals is important, but there is nothing in Christian teaching that would particularly support vegetarianism. Jesus declared all foods clean (Mark 7:19) and permitted the eating of all meat. On these grounds, some Christians may consider it unbiblical to adopt vegetarianism or veganism, or to limit the diet in any way not directly related to improving or maintaining health. However, in another book of the Bible St Paul claimed that while all foods were permitted to Christians, they should avoid eating anything in a situation that would distress another Christian or lead them to **sin**: 'Food will not bring us close to God. We are no worse off if we do not eat, and no better off if we do. But take care that this liberty of yours does not somehow become a stumbling block to the weak' (1 Corinthians 8:8–9).

Christians have traditionally taught that animals do not have the same rights as human beings. Humans were given dominion (authority) over animals at creation (Genesis 1:28), and only humans have rights because they alone, not animals, were made in the image of God. Although farmers, scientists and those who care for animals should treat them kindly, it is acceptable to use them for the benefit of humans, particularly, as in the case of animal experimentation, where there is no alternative. Unlike Judaism and Islam, Christianity has no religious rules for slaughtering animals, although animals should be killed in a humane way.

- Augustine argued that all commands concerning the welfare of animals were essentially for the benefit of humans, for example resting cattle on the Sabbath so they are fresh to resume work.
- Aquinas claimed humans have no duties to animals, and should only treat them with care so that cruel treatment does not carry over into cruel treatment of humans.
- Descartes regarded animals as machines like clocks, which move and make sounds, but have no feelings.
- Kant held that animals were not ends in themselves, and so the only reason for being kind to them was to practise being kind to humans.

Nevertheless, some Christians believe that because animals are as much a part of God's creation as human beings, they should be treated in exactly the same way. Jesus taught that God's care for animals and birds should show humans his care for them: 'Are not five sparrows sold for a penny? Yet not one of them is forgotten by God' (Luke 12:6). Thus, if the life of animals is important to God, it should be important to humans too and it is part of human calling to stewardship to care for animals, not to exploit them. Some argue that is impossible to raise animals for food or use them for experimentation without being cruel to them, and so these actions cannot be justified.

Islamic views

> There is not a beast in the earth whose sustenance does not depend on Allah. He knows its dwelling and its resting place.
> (Surah 11:6)

> Eat the lawful and good food which Allah has provided for you.... He has forbidden only carrion, blood and swine flesh.
> (Surah 16:114–115)

Islam also teaches that animals are part of Allah's creation and, as his Khalifahs, humans are required to respect them. Unlike Christianity, Islam also teaches that animals have feelings and a purpose in their lives and so must be killed painlessly. The Qur'an allows the eating of **halal** (permitted) animals for food, and the Shari'ah Law permits the use of animals for experimentation.

There is not an animal that lives on the earth, nor a being that flies on its wings, but forms part of communities like you. Nothing have we omitted from the Book, and they all shall be gathered to their Lord in the end.

(Surah 6:38)

See you not that it is God whose praises all beings in the heavens and on earth do celebrate. And the birds of the air with wings outspread? Each one knows its own mode of prayer and praise. And God knows well all that they do.

(Surah 24:41)

Animals used for farming and other industries should be properly looked after and it is not part of Islam to make them work until they are dropping with exhaustion or their flesh is damaged. Islam also rejects hunting and killing animals for sport or recreation. The only legitimate reason to kill animals is for food.

If someone kills even a sparrow for sport, the sparrow will cry out on the Day of Judgement, 'O Lord! That person killed me for nothing! He did not kill me for any useful purpose!'

(Hadith)

A butcher cuts meat at a halal food market

Animals used for hunting should be well trained and not encouraged to be savage, and, in turn, when humans hunt animals for food, they should use sharp, not blunt, weapons because these are more humane. Dog fights, cock fights, bull fighting, fox hunting and bear baiting are all forbidden within Islam and no Muslim could support killing animals for their fur, skin, tusks or horns. Only if an animal is killed for food can its other products be used, so as not to be wasteful.

Islam forbids cruel farming methods such as battery farming or force-feeding animals to modify the flavour of their flesh or increase its fat content. Most importantly, all animal products must be from animals that have been slaughtered by a halal butcher. In Muslim countries, all men are trained how to slaughter an animal by this method, and in the West halal butchers provide meat that has come from correctly slaughtered animals. Some supermarkets in the UK sell halal meat products because it is not permissible for anyone to slaughter animals on private premises. Halal meat is killed so that the animal feels as little pain as possible, using a very sharp knife drawn across the jugular vein. The animal loses consciousness almost immediately and the blood drains away easily so humans do not eat it. Prayers are said throughout the slaughter. An animal should not be slaughtered in front of another one, and it should not be denied food or water because it is about to be slaughtered.

> Neither the flesh of the animals of your sacrifice nor their blood reaches Allah — it is your righteousness that reaches him.
>
> (Surah 22:37)

Questions and activities

Sample questions and answers

1 What does the word 'conservation' mean? (2 marks)

Conservation is the process of preserving and maintaining the environment.

2 Why do Christians believe it is important to protect the environment? (6 marks)

Christians believe they have a responsibility to be stewards of the environment. The concept of stewardship is the view that the earth was created by God and given to human beings to care for and protect. This is clearly set out in the creation narratives in Genesis: 'God blessed them, and said to them "Be fruitful and multiply. Rule over the fish of the sea and the birds of the air and over every living thing that moves on the ground"' (Genesis 1:28). This means that God gave man authority over the earth, which is supposed to be used wisely and compassionately. God also gave man the responsibility to 'till the earth and keep it' (Genesis 2:15). This clearly suggests that the earth will not look after itself, and if he is to benefit from it he must look after it.

Polluting the planet is not responsible stewardship, and draining natural resources is selfish and greedy and abuses the gifts of God in creation, which are given for all generations, not just the present one. Therefore, Christians believe they have a responsibility to work towards reducing pollution and cutting back on use of non-renewable resources, to share natural resources more fairly, and to support environmental groups.

3 Explain the views of Christians concerning animal rights.

(8 marks)

Christians believe animals are part of God's creation and so are subject to the same principles of stewardship that apply to the rest of the natural world. Humans were put in charge of animals at creation, and so are responsible for treating them humanely and compassionately. However, Christianity does not teach vegetarianism since Jesus declared all foods permissible. Some Christians may choose to be vegetarian, but others may consider it to be unbiblical, since God provided all foods for human benefit. Unlike Judaism and Islam, Christianity has no religious rules for slaughtering animals, although animals should be killed in a humane way.

Christians have traditionally taught that animals do not have the same rights as human beings since only humans were made in the image of God. For example, Aquinas claimed humans have no duties to animals, and should only treat them with care so that cruel treatment does not carry over into cruel treatment of humans. Although farmers, scientists and those who care for animals should treat them kindly, it is legitimate to use them for the benefit of humans, particularly in the case of animal experimentation where there is no alternative.

However, some Christians argue that since it is impossible to eat animals, or use them for experimentation or as part of sport, without causing them some pain, these actions can never be justified. Jesus taught that God's care for animals and birds should reassure humans of his care for them: 'Are not five sparrows sold for a penny? Yet not one of them is forgotten by God' (Luke 12:6). Thus, if the life of animals is important to God, it should be important to humans too.

---

4 'Religious believers should make concern for the environment a priority.' Do you agree? Give reasons for your opinion, showing you have considered other points of view.

(4 marks)

Since most religions teach that the earth is precious and made by God out of his love and power, there seems to be no good reason for religious believers not to put concern for the environment high among their priorities. God's gifts in creation are for the benefit of all humans, and not just for the present generation, so religious believers should consider it important to ensure that future generations can look forward to an environment that is as beautiful and full of natural resources as we enjoy today. Already, many parts of the world have been spoiled by human greed and lack of understanding about how to care for the environment, but there is still a lot that religious believers can do to improve the state of the world and to preserve it for the future.

However, some may argue that although care for the environment is a good and important thing, it should not be prioritised over and above other things. Some religious believers are concerned when they see people giving more care to environmental and animal rights campaigns than they think should be given, on the grounds that care for humans must always take precedence. Nevertheless, it is worth considering that unless we do take care of the environment, humans will suffer, so to make it a priority helps everyone either immediately or in the future. Caring for the earth is, indirectly, caring for other human beings too.

Further questions

1 What does the word 'stewardship' mean?   (2 marks)
2 Outline the teachings of one religion other than Christianity on care for
   the environment.   (6 marks)
3 Explain why religious believers may have different views on animal
   rights.   (8 marks)
4 'Eating meat is a God-given right.' Do you agree? Give reasons for your
   opinion, showing you have considered other points of view. In your
   answer, you should refer to Christianity and one other religion.   (4 marks)

Class activities and homework

Understanding pollution

Your teacher will divide the class into small groups and ask each group to set up an imaginary industrial manufacturing company. Devise a set of environmentally friendly, pollution-free rules that you would apply to your company. Identify some of the problems of implementing these rules and how they may be of long-term or short-term benefit to (a) the company, (b) the immediate environment and (c) raising awareness of the dangers of pollution. Share your views with the rest of the class and then vote on which group has come up with the most practical suggestions.

Using the internet, find out about one international pollution disaster. Prepare a fact sheet for the rest of the class and suggest ways in which religious groups might respond to the disaster.

Understanding care for the environment

Explore some of the claims that have been made against the fast-food chain, McDonald's, on environmental grounds. A good place to start is *Fast Food Nation* by Eric Schlosser (Penguin, 2002). Your teacher will summarise the key points for you. As a class, try to reach some conclusions about these issues, concentrating on whether religious believers should make a stand against fast-food organisations that may be guilty of putting profits before the environment.

'Religious believers do not do enough to protect the environment. They are too interested in heaven to look after the earth.' Do you agree? Give reasons for your opinion, showing you have considered other points of view.

Understanding animal rights

In pairs or small groups, on a large sheet of paper, draw a diagram or make a table summarising as many arguments as possible for and against animal experimentation and the use of animals for human purposes. Then, in your pairs or groups, answer the following question: 'The use of animals in ways that cause them harm, or do not respect their rights, can never be justified by religion.' Share your views with the rest of the class.

Find out about one manufacturing company, such as The Body Shop, which campaigns against animal testing. Prepare a fact sheet for the rest of the class.

Religion: peace and conflict

Conflict in the world today

One of the most important tasks of any state is to ensure the safety of its citizens, both as individuals and as members of society. That is why countries have laws to protect individuals from being hurt by others in society, and why they have military forces to protect their citizens from conflict with other nations and groups.

There are always armed conflicts going on in the world. The United Nations (UN) was established in 1945 to bring countries together so that there would never be another world war. The aim of the UN has always been to remove the causes of war, but it has had only limited success. The causes of war are many and varied. War can be caused by disputes over land, water, energy and oil, or through more ancient and deep-rooted arguments involving religion, ethnic origin and national identity.

Nuclear weapons and weapons of mass destruction

Nuclear weapons and other **weapons of mass destruction** pose a great threat to **world peace** because they can cause huge destruction and tremendous loss of life.

Nuclear weapons, such as atomic bombs, are based on atomic fission or fusion. The atomic bomb dropped on Hiroshima in 1945 killed 140,000 people, yet the uranium inside it could have been contained in a cricket ball. Today's bombs are much more powerful. Although there has been a decrease in the number of atomic weapons since the end of the Cold War in the late 1980s, there are still about 20,000 nuclear warheads in existence, of which the USA has about 10,000. The UK is thought to have around 200. Russia, France, China, Israel, India and Pakistan also possess nuclear weapons.

Nuclear test, 1956

Any act of war aimed indiscriminately at the destruction of entire cities or of extensive areas along with their population is a crime against God and man himself.

(Second Vatican Council)

Other weapons of mass destruction are non-nuclear weapons that can destroy large areas and kill great numbers of people. There are two main types of weapon: chemical and biological. Chemical weapons include poison gas, which Saddam Hussein used with devastating effect against Iraqi Kurds in the Iran–Iraq War. Biological weapons, which so far have not been used in modern warfare, include diseases such as anthrax, botulis, smallpox and plague. One of the causes of the war in Iraq was the belief that Saddam Hussein had stockpiled large quantities of such weapons. However, an intensive search of Iraq by weapons inspectors failed to find any such weapons.

The war in Iraq

The Iraq War began on 20 March 2003, when coalition forces led by the USA launched an attack against Iraq. The aim of the war, according to President George W. Bush, was to 'disarm Iraq and to free its people'.

The threat of war had been building up for a long time. The First Gulf War a decade earlier had left the authoritarian regime of Saddam Hussein intact.

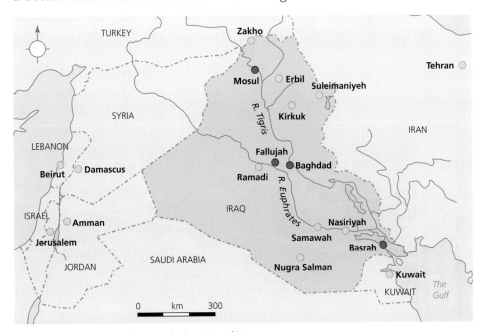

Map of the Middle East showing the location of Iraq

Bush and his allies believed Saddam Hussein had links with terrorist networks, including al-Qaeda, and had been stockpiling weapons of mass destruction that presented a serious threat to the safety of the Western world.

The UN did not endorse the attack on Iraq, and some key UN members such as France, Russia and China strongly opposed the use of force. In the event, the USA's principal allies (known as the coalition) were the UK and Australia.

The war itself lasted only a few weeks. It began with a missile attack on Saddam Hussein's headquarters and, soon after, coalition troops seized the Iraqi oilfields in the north. There was continued precision bombing of Baghdad by the coalition and fierce fighting between troops of both sides in the central and southern regions of Iraq.

By 2 April, Iraq's elite force, the Republican Guard, had been largely defeated. On 7 April, British troops attacked the second city of Basrah, taking control 2 days later. In the north, American forces, alongside local Kurdish fighters, seized the cities of Mosul and Kirkuk. However, with no local police force left, these cities became chaotic, and looting and violence spread.

By 4 April, allied troops had captured Saddam International Airport in Baghdad and the next day US bombers attacked government buildings in

The lack of law and order following the fall of the Iraq government led to widespread violence and looting

Baghdad. A US infantry battalion drove through Baghdad on a raid, killing over 1,000 Iraqis. American forces surrounded the Iraqi capital and began their assault on 8 April. The Iraqi government fell the next day and the giant statue of Saddam Hussein that stood in the city square was soon torn down by local people. Most of the fighting then stopped and the American forces took control of the city, following this up by capturing Saddam Hussein's home town of Tikrit.

At this time it seemed that most Iraqis were pleased to see the end of Saddam Hussein's regime, but small groups of Iraqi paramilitaries and Saddam loyalists continued to fight. The lack of law and order meant there was widespread violence and looting as there was no central structure or coordination. The coalition troops were faced with the huge task of restoring Iraq, maintaining law and order, and repairing the damage, as well as ensuring that the people received electricity, fresh water, food, medical aid and supplies. President Bush declared an end to combat operations on 1 May.

However, it proved difficult to bring peace to Iraq. Iraqi paramilitaries continued to attack coalition troops, disrupt services and use car bombs to cause death and destruction. Meanwhile, criticism against the war grew in the rest of the world, particularly because no weapons of mass destruction had been found either during or after the war. In September 2003, President Bush admitted that there was no evidence to link Saddam's regime with the terrorist group al-Qaeda, which had been responsible for the terrorist attacks in the USA on 11 September 2001. The situation was made worse by reports of US and UK military and civilian personnel apparently abusing Iraqi prisoners.

On 22 July 2003, Saddam's sons Uday and Qusay were killed in a battle in the city of Mosul. By September, the coalition forces had managed to calm the situation in the south of the country and in Mosul in the north. However, it was more difficult to bring about order in the central region around Baghdad and there were many bombings by Iraqi fighters, including explosions at a UN compound on 19 August and the assassinations of prominent leaders. On 13 December 2003, US forces finally captured Saddam Hussein himself, hiding in a small cellar in a farmhouse near Tikrit.

However, the unrest in Iraq continued and a number of Western workers were kidnapped, some of whom were later executed by Islamic militant fighters. At the centre of the unrest was the city of Fallujah and, in 2004, US forces had to lay siege to the city and occupy it. The occupation of Iraq was very unpopular in the West. President Bush and Prime Minister Tony Blair were put under great pressure to take their troops out of Iraq. Conflict in this region is likely to continue for several years to come.

The Arab–Israeli conflict

The origins of this conflict lie in the distant past. Palestine, the historic land of the Jews, had been conquered many times by invaders. In 135 CE, the Romans finally expelled the Jews from the land. In the centuries that followed, the land was populated by Muslim Arabs, who became known as Palestinians.

Map showing the frontiers after the 1967 war

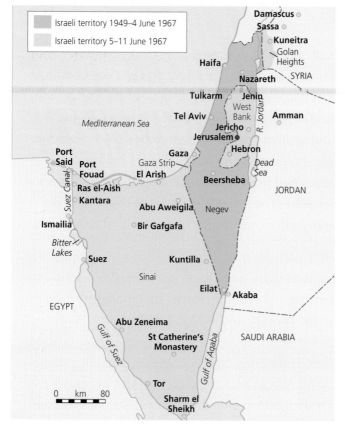

In the 1890s, a Jewish journalist called Theodor Herzl began a campaign for Jews to return to Palestine, because the Jews were 'a people without a land and a land without a people'.

The Zionist movement, as it became known, grew in strength and many Jews living in Europe moved to Palestine. They bought a great deal of land from the Arabs who lived there, and established major settlements.

After the First World War, the British had temporary control over Palestine and promised both the Jews and the Arabs that they would have their own land. The promise to the Jews was contained in the Balfour Declaration, which said: 'His Majesty's government view with favour the establishment in Palestine of a national home for the Jewish people.'

In 1922, the British separated Palestine into two parts. The land to the east of the River Jordan became the Emirate of Transjordan (now called Jordan), and the land to the west was Palestine. However, this immediately led to conflict between Jews and Arabs in Palestine, who fought over who should have control over the government, land and economy.

The conflict remained unresolved for several years. After the Second World War and the Holocaust, in which millions of Jews died, world opinion began to favour the creation of an independent Jewish state. In 1947, the UN passed Resolution 181, calling for Palestine to be divided into separate Jewish and Arab states. On 14 May 1948, the British withdrew and the Jewish state, now named Israel, declared its independence. Almost immediately, Israel was attacked by Palestinians and Arabs from the surrounding countries and war followed.

Against the odds, Israel defeated the Arab forces and expanded the land under its control. A large number of Palestinians found themselves as refugees with no land or home. The Arab states refused to accept the refugees, and so the conflict between Jews and Palestinians continued.

The Six-Day War between Israel and the surrounding Arab nations broke out in 1967. Israel was again victorious and seized more land, and, in the process, more Palestinians became refugees. The Arab states called for the destruction of Israel and a campaign of terrorism followed, led by the Palestinian Liberation Organisation (PLO). In 1973, the Arab nations again attacked Israel (the Arab–Israeli War). Once again, Israel was victorious, but the price in lives and materials was heavy.

The wars had taken their toll on both sides and, in 1977, the Egyptian President Anwar al-Sadat met with the Israeli Prime Minister Manachem and US President Carter to negotiate peace. This agreement became known as the Camp David Accords. However, the other Arab nations refused to agree and unrest and terrorism continued, particularly against Syria and in the Lebanon, where Israel repeatedly attacked PLO bases.

In the late 1980s, the Palestinians began an uprising to protest against the Israeli occupation of the main areas where they lived — the Gaza Strip and the West Bank. Riots and terrorism followed and many were killed on both sides. Pressure was placed on Israel from many outside nations to make some compromises with the Palestinians. After the First Gulf War of 1991, the USA — Israel's strongest ally — invited both the Arabs and the Israelis to come to the Madrid Peace Conference to try to work out a peaceful agreement.

Yasser Arafat, Bill Clinton and Yitzak Rabin in Oslo

Little was achieved, but 2 years later a significant step forward was taken when both sides met in Oslo. The Oslo Accords, as the agreement was called, provided for a gradual transfer of power to the Palestinians, giving them authority in the Gaza Strip and the West Bank. The PLO leader Yasser Arafat was made the first president. Following this, Israel made a peaceful settlement with its neighbour, Jordan, and some dialogue with other Arab nations also began.

However, terrorism and bloodshed continued on both sides and the Israeli Prime Minister Yitzhak Rabin was assassinated in 1995. Israeli troops left the West Bank under the new Prime Minister Benjamin Netanyahu but Jews continued to build homes and settlements in Arab East Jerusalem, causing anger to the Palestinians and the outside world.

In 1998, Israel signed an agreement with the Palestinians whereby Israeli troops would leave the West Bank, provided the Palestinians stopped terrorist attacks on Israel. However, both sides claimed the other was not carrying out the agreement. The following year, a new Israeli Prime Minister, Ehud Barak, entered into negotiations with Yasser Arafat, aided by US President Clinton, but the two sides were unable to agree.

Both sides were angry and frustrated and a second uprising broke out in September 2000 after Israeli opposition leader Ariel Sharon made a tour of the al-Aqsa complex in Jerusalem, which enraged Palestinians. Violence erupted in the West Bank and Gaza Strip, as well as suicide bombings and terrorist attacks in Israel, and many hundreds of lives were lost.

In 2001, Ariel Sharon was elected prime minister of Israel. He took a hard line against the Palestinians by ordering the assassination of their leaders and ordered air strikes into Palestinian territory. He also refused to speak to Yasser Arafat and the bitterness between both sides continued. In November 2004, Yasser Arafat died and a new Palestinian leadership was elected. Whether or not such new leadership will bring a lasting peace with Israel remains to be seen.

Religious attitudes to war

Christian views

> You have heard that it was said, 'Love your neighbour and hate your enemy.' But I tell you: Love your enemies and pray for those who persecute you.
>
> (Matthew 5:43–44)

One of the most important things that Jesus taught and which Christians try to follow is the concept of peace on earth. The New Testament is filled with teachings concerning peace and how Christians should learn to love all people and bring peace and **reconciliation** in times of trouble.

Key word

Reconciliation
Bringing people back together after a dispute

> Blessed are the peacemakers, for they will be called sons of God.
>
> (Matthew 5:9)

The Christian Churches have also made statements about the need for peace, encouraging Christians to seek peace and not war.

> Peace is very much at the heart of the teaching of Jesus, yet Christians have long been divided about whether it is ever right to go to war or use violence. All believe that war is wrong, but some believe that there are times when a Christian just has to go to war. This is because they believe that the result of not going to war will be much worse.
>
> (Church of England report 'Peacemaking in a Nuclear Age')

The only legitimate purpose of nuclear deterrence is to prevent war. It is therefore immoral to procure or deploy more weapons than are needed simply to deter a potential aggressor from starting a war. Any quest for 'superiority' is forbidden.

(Catechism of the Catholic Church)

Key word

Pacifism
Refusing to fight in a war

However, the Bible does not state clearly whether or not Christians should fight in a war and attitudes within the Church are not always the same. In the early Church, the principle of total **pacifism** was adopted, but this changed some centuries later when pacifist Christians were accused of weakening the defences of the Roman empire.

Today, there are two main viewpoints that Christians adopt concerning what they should do if war breaks out.

Christians and pacifism

Pacifism means refusing to fight in a war. There are different types of pacifism, ranging from total or absolute pacifism — which means no engagement in military activity at all — to relative, selective or nuclear pacifism — which means no engagement in military activity in certain circumstances, such as the use of nuclear weapons.

Anti-war protestors

From the start of Christianity 2,000 years ago, many Christians have refused to fight, saying that Jesus taught that fighting was wrong: 'But I tell you, do not resist an evil person. If someone strikes you on the right cheek, turn to him the other also' (Matthew 5:39). In modern times, Christian groups, such as the Quakers, the Plymouth Brethren and the Catholic organisation Pax Christi, have refused to engage in any kind of violent struggle and have declared that they will not resist those who attack them:

Quakers are (for the most part) pacifist; they do not join armies and in times of conscription are conscientious objectors. It is not just a negative witness — not just a refusal to use or participate in violence — but a positive commitment to peacemaking and peace building.

(Quaker publication, *Advices and Queries*)

There are five main reasons why Christians might choose pacifism:

- The Ten Commandments forbid killing: 'You shall not commit murder' (Exodus 20:13).
- Jesus taught that people should love their enemies.
- Jesus stopped his own followers from using violence. When Peter drew a sword to fight, Jesus said: 'Put your sword back in its place…for all who draw the sword will die by the sword' (Matthew 26:52).
- If people act peacefully towards each other, eventually peace will be established.
- Nuclear weapons and weapons of mass destruction can cause unimaginable suffering.

War is contrary to the spirit, teaching and purpose of Christ.

(Methodist statement on peace and war)

Christians and just war

Not all Christians agree with pacifism. There are many who believe that wars, however undesirable and awful, sometimes have to be fought. It was Augustine who first put forward the principles that are now called **just war**. He laid down certain conditions, which, if fulfilled, would justify Christians fighting in a war. These proposals covered the reasons for resorting to war (*jus ad bellum*) and the conduct of the war itself (*jus in bello*). These principles are recognised now by most Christian Churches and have been used to justify many recent wars, including the Falklands, the Gulf Wars, and the troubles in Bosnia, Kosovo and elsewhere.

Key word

Just war
The basis upon which a Christian can decide when it is right to go to war. It refers to a war that is fought in a right way and for the right reasons

Under the just war criteria, a Christian can fight in a war if:

- the cause of the war is 'just', such as resisting aggression and injustice
- the war is fought with the authority of the government or UN
- it is fought with the right intention, where the aim is to bring peace

- it is a last resort, after all negotiations and non-violent methods of solving the dispute have failed
- there is a reasonable likelihood of success and lives will not be wasted in vain; it ought to lead to a better state of affairs than existed before
- warfare is discriminate and civilians are not targeted
- the methods used are reasonably proportionate between the injustice being fought and the suffering that is inflicted, for example not using nuclear weapons against a non-nuclear nation

> The use of nuclear weapons cannot be justified. Such weapons cannot be used without harming non-combatants, and could never be proportionate to the just cause and aim of war.... In our view the cause of right cannot be upheld by fighting a nuclear war.
> (Church of England unofficial report, 'The Church and the Bomb')

> Any policy for security which includes nuclear deterrence must be compatible with, and indeed promote, human rights, cooperation and international trust on which alone a secure peace can be built.
> (Catechism of the Catholic Church)

Christians say there is teaching in the Bible to support the just war theory. For example:

- Jesus told the people they should obey the lawful government: 'Give to Caesar what is Caesar's and to God what is God's' (Mark 12:17).
- Paul told people that Christians have a duty to obey those in authority: 'Everyone must submit himself to the governing authorities, for there is no authority except that which God has established' (Romans 13:1).

President Bush used religious ideas to great effect when talking about the Iraq conflict

Moreover, they claim that just as countries have police forces to protect them from criminals, it is also right to have armed forces to protect the nation from outside enemy aggressors.

> As long as the danger of war persists... governments cannot be denied the right of lawful self-defence, once all peace efforts have failed.
> (Catechism of the Catholic Church)

However, the notion of just war has often been used by leaders and interpreted in their own way. For example, President George W. Bush is supposed to have said: 'God told me to strike at al-Qaeda and I struck them, and then he instructed me to strike at Saddam, which I did.' Politically, Bush has used religious ideas to great effect when talking about the Iraq conflict, defining America as good and its enemies or targets as evil. On 12 September 2001, Bush declared: 'This will be a monumental struggle of good versus evil, but good will prevail'. Bush later defined America's enemies as the 'axis of evil'.

Islamic views

> Fight in the cause of God those who fight you, but do not transgress the limits; for God loves not the transgressors.
>
> (Surah 2:190)

The Qur'an teaches that Muslims should be prepared to struggle or strive in the way of Islam. The word 'strive' in Arabic is 'jihad'. For Muslims, the most important struggle they must undertake is the greater, or inner, jihad, which is a struggle they fight within themselves. It is a spiritual and emotional fight rather than a physical one, and the aim is to become truly submitted to Allah. Inner jihad involves change in one's self and mentality. It may concern the sacrifice of material property, social class and emotional comfort for the sake of Allah alone. Examples of inner jihad would be to exceed in good deeds, to visit the mosque often, to study the scripture in detail, to help poor people and orphans, to stand up for people's right for freedom, to be fair, never to bear false testimony, and to stay on good terms with friends and neighbours. It also involves controlling sinful desires such as adultery, stealing, lying, cheating, insulting people and taking part in gossip. When Muslims are successful in inner jihad, they are at peace and achieve a level of surrender that enables them to fulfil the will of Allah. As a result, the Muslim who practises jihad will gain tremendously in the afterlife.

Nevertheless, the meaning the Western media often give to jihad is false. The media have encouraged people to be afraid of Muslim violence. This has led to mosque committees fearing closure, as in the case of the Finsbury Park Mosque in north London. Misunderstandings of Islam are not new. They can be traced back 1,000 years to the Crusades when Islam was spreading quickly to the West and was thought to be a threat to the status of the Christian Church. In the modern world, anti-Muslim feeling in the Western media, particularly in the USA, is, according to some people, a reaction to the downfall of the Soviet Union, which, they argue, left the West seeking a new enemy to fear.

The lesser jihad is about the physical struggle against enemies of Islam. According to Islam and the Qur'an, there is no such thing as a holy war. However, there are certain circumstances in which Islam tolerates and sometimes even accepts the practice of war. Islam strongly emphasises the ideas of justice, freedom and opposition to oppression, and will permit fighting in self-defence. War is tolerated in these conditions, but if there is a reasonable possibility of avoiding war, this alternative must be taken.

Muslims believe they can fight in a war to defend their faith because:
- the Qur'an teaches that Muslims must fight if they are attacked
- Muhammad himself fought in wars
- many of the statements of Muhammad (Hadith) permit Muslims to fight in just wars
- the Qur'an teaches that anyone who dies in a just war will go to heaven

> Think not of those who are slain in God's way. Nay, they live, finding their sustenance in the presence of the Lord.
>
> (Surah 3:169)

There are strict rules about when Muslims can justifiably fight in a military jihad. It must be fought for a just cause — that is, in defence of Islam. This can include self-defence and fighting injustice.

- It must be a last resort after non-violent methods have failed.
- It must be authorised by a Muslim authority — this can be a spiritual leader who understands the situation and acts fairly.
- It must be fought with the minimum of suffering.
- Innocent civilians must not be attacked. Trees, crops and animals should be left undamaged.
- It must end when the enemy surrenders and prisoners of the war should be released.
- It should aim to restore peace and freedom.

Muslims can, therefore, fight any enemy that threatens the Islamic faith and a Muslim soldier must be prepared to die for his faith.

However, just as in Christianity, a skilful leader can often use the notion of a just war for their own purposes. For example, after the destruction of the World Trade Center in New York on 11 September 2001, Osama bin Laden said: 'I swear by Almighty God…that neither the United States nor he who lives in the United States will enjoy security before…all the infidel armies leave the land of Muhammad'. The events of 11 September led to very strong reactions worldwide, some aimed at America, others at Islamic extremism. Many Muslims who did not support the attacks found themselves the targets of violent prejudice.

A programme shown on Channel 4 in January 2004, called *Turning Muslim in Texas*, revealed that since the attacks on the World Trade Center in 2001 there had been an increasing interest in Islam among Americans seeking to find out what the religion really teaches and not just how the popular media and political opportunists want to present it. There are now 400,000 Muslims in Texas alone, a number of whom have converted since 11 September 2001. In the programme, David, a white American who converted to Islam while in the US army, suggested that becoming a Muslim could save Americans from themselves and that if President George W. Bush converted, it would discourage him from some of his 'ill-advised imperial adventures overseas'.

Osama bin Laden

The work of those seeking world peace

There are a number of groups and individuals which work hard campaigning for world peace and the removal of the causes of war. Some of the most well known non-religious groups are:

- The United Nations (UN): established in 1945 with the aim of keeping the world peaceful and making sure there would never be another world war. It states that it works to 'unite our strength to maintain international peace'.

CND march

- The Campaign for Nuclear Disarmament (CND): this organisation campaigns to rid the world of nuclear weapons and weapons of mass destruction.
- The European Nuclear Disarmament Campaign: this organisation calls upon nations with nuclear weapons to disarm.
- The World Disarmament Campaign: set up in 1980 with the aim of putting pressure on governments around the world to give up the use of weapons.
- Amnesty International: an organisation that campaigns for peace and helps those who have suffered as a result of war, torture and abuse of human rights.

Religious workers for peace

As well as these organisations, there are a number of religious groups, communities and individuals which campaign for world peace.

The World Council of Churches (WCC)

The WCC is an organisation that brings together Christians from different Churches and denominations all over the world, representing nearly 400 million Christians. One of its aims is to work for world peace through discussion and dialogue. It tries to build bridges between peoples who are divided by religious and historical conflict.

The WCC was established in 1948 and seeks to get Christians of all denominations to work together to teach about God and to heal the divisions and conflicts between peoples of different nations and beliefs. In particular, members of the WCC follow the teachings of Jesus concerning the need for peace among all people. They strive to break down the barriers between people, they campaign for justice and peace, and they try to establish a unity of peace among all peoples.

The Churches that make up the WCC are from different social, economic, cultural and political backgrounds. Each has agreed to help the others in time of need and to work together in a peaceful and productive way. The WCC supports individual and national Churches that are involved in struggles in their known countries. For example, in its Programme to Combat Racism, the WCC worked for peace and justice in the struggle against apartheid in South Africa. It has also been involved in conflicts in Sudan and Korea, and campaigned against military dictatorships in Latin America.

Pax Christi

Pax Christi (Latin for 'the peace of Christ') is an international Catholic peace organisation, based on the principles taught by Jesus. It was set up in 1945, originally to work for reconciliation between French and German Catholics after the Second World War. It has since grown into a worldwide organisation. Pax Christi is opposed to war and all forms of violence. It campaigns for governments to solve their disputes with other nations through dialogue, and economic and social justice. It has three objectives:

Pax Christi activists

- reconciliation
- peace
- education and learning

Key word

Forgiveness
Ending a dispute with someone and not blaming them for what has gone wrong

> Our vision is of a world where people can live in peace and without fear of violence in all its forms. We believe in the power of prayer, reconciliation, **forgiveness**, justice and non-violence and the right to live in a culture which promotes these values and treats the whole of God's creation in a respectful and just manner.
>
> (Pax Christi website)

The groups around the world that make up Pax Christi work in a non-violent way campaigning for peace. They do this by:

- informing Catholics of the teachings of Jesus concerning peace
- engaging in public discussion and debate about issues of war and peace (Pax Christi campaigned against the wars in Iraq, Yugoslavia and Africa)
- criticising governments over how much they spend on weapons and defence

- organising public awareness of the moral issues surrounding nuclear weapons and weapons of mass destruction
- campaigning against abuses of human rights and the causes of war
- trying to establish international teams who can intervene in areas of conflict and secure peace

> As for ourselves, we confess how often we have been silent while those considered our enemies have been attacked. Forgive us for the times our hearts have been cold as they suffered. We ask above all else that you help us respond in the way we have been shown by your son, Jesus.
>
> (Pax Christi prayer for peace)

Islamic Relief and the Muslim Peace Fellowship

The promotion of peace and freedom is central to the teachings of Islam

Islamic Relief was founded in 1984 and was the first Muslim relief agency in Europe. It works all over the world campaigning and helping those suffering as a result of war. In recent years, it has worked in Bosnia, Somalia and Iraq. Alongside this organisation, the Muslim Peace Fellowship works to promote world peace. It was founded in 1994 and is described as: 'a gathering of peace and justice-orientated Muslims of all backgrounds who are dedicated to making the beauty of Islam evident in the world'.

Both organisations are firmly based on Islamic principles because the protection of human rights and the promotion of peace and freedom are central to the teachings of Islam: 'Whoever saved a life, it would be as if he saved the life of all mankind' (Surah 5:32).

Neve Shalom/Wahat al-Salam

Neve Shalom/Wahat al-Salam is a peace village in the heart of Israel. It was founded in 1970 by Bruno Hussar, a Dominican monk. He wanted to create a place where Jews and Palestinians could live together in peace, despite their differences. The name means 'oasis of peace' and today Jews, Christians and Muslims live and work there together in peace. It has a primary school and a school for peace and welcomes visitors from all lands and faiths.

Bruce Kent

Bruce Kent is one of the world's most famous Christian campaigners for world peace. He was born in 1929 and is best known for his work with the Campaign for Nuclear Disarmament (CND), an organisation in which he served as general secretary from 1980 to 1985 and then as chairman from 1987 to 1990. He campaigned against nuclear weapons because he believed that life was a sacred gift from God and that it was wrong to threaten to kill millions of people using nuclear weapons or weapons of mass destruction. He worked for CND because it campaigned in a non-violent way, and he tried throughout his life to convince people of the need to consider alternatives to nuclear weapons and settling disputes by military action. He was a constant critic of UK government policy and sought to eliminate nuclear weapons throughout the world.

Bruce Kent

Kent was a Catholic priest with the title of Monsignor, but in 1987 he came into conflict with Cardinal Hume, the leader of Britain's Catholics at that time, who instructed him not to campaign against nuclear weapons during the general election campaign. Kent refused to comply and was forced to resign from his position in the Church. Today, he still campaigns for world peace and is now the honorary vice president of CND.

Bullying

As well as conflict between different nations, there is conflict between individual people and one of the most common kinds of conflict is **bullying**. Bullies frighten or intimidate people whom they see as being weaker than themselves. Bullies can be individuals or people acting as a group. Often bullies are older or stronger than those they are bullying. A lot of bullying happens in schools and it can result in victims staying away from school, being upset, injured, ill, depressed and, rarely, committing suicide.

Key word

Bullying
Hurting, frightening, intimidating or humiliating another person

Examples of bullying include:

- physical bullying and causing deliberate physical harm
- calling people names
- telling lies against people
- stealing or damaging someone else's property
- accusing people of things they have not done in order to get them into trouble or damage their reputation
- racist bullying: physically or verbally attacking someone on the grounds of their race, colour or culture

Bullies frighten or intimidate people

Every year, ten or more children commit suicide as a result of having been bullied, and one in twelve children is bullied so badly that it affects their education.

Among adults, bullying can happen at work, if people in authority, for example, use their power to frighten or humiliate others. Such bullying is usually mental rather than physical, but it can still result in upset, mental illness and, in extreme cases, suicide.

People become bullies for a number of reasons. Among the most common are:

- problems at home
- having been a victim of bullying themselves
- wanting to look tough
- having low self-esteem, which they take out on their victims

Religious attitudes to bullying

All religions condemn bullying on the grounds that using physical or mental violence and oppression without just cause, if indeed there can be any just cause, is wrong. Religions all claim that every human being is precious and the creation of God. Believers feel it matters to God how people behave and how they treat one another. Jesus taught about the love of God for all his creation and believers say it is the duty of all Christians to follow this teaching in their own lives. In particular, protecting the weak and innocent is part of God's teaching. Furthermore, both the Old and New Testaments teach that taking revenge, even against cruel behaviour, is not the responsibility of the believer but of God.

> Do not seek revenge or bear a grudge against one of your people, but love your neighbour as yourself.
>
> (Leviticus 19:18)

> If someone hits you on the right cheek, offer him your left also…and if someone forces you to go one mile, go with him two miles.
>
> (Matthew 5:39,41)

> Let there arise out of you a band of people inviting to all that is good, enjoining what is right, and forbidding what is wrong.
>
> (Surah 3:104)

Non-religious attitudes to bullying

Most people are opposed to bullying and the law protects the victims of physical and mental harm. Verbal bullying is an offence called assault and can carry a prison sentence of up to 6 months. Physical violence can be an offence of battery or even worse, such as causing grievous bodily harm, which can carry a prison sentence of many years.

The law is based on the principle that everyone has human rights and therefore has the right to live their lives free from fear of being hurt by others. Society is based on respect for others and cannot function properly if bullies are allowed to get away with intimidating and hurting others.

In schools, there are anti-bullying policies. The victims of bullying can report any actions taken against them to someone in authority who can deal with the situation. For adults in the workplace, the trade unions have rules and procedures to help the victims of bullying.

The Department for Education and Skills (DfES) ran the first anti-bullying week from 22 to 26 November 2004. During this time, it launched an anti-bullying video featuring Rio Ferdinand, Vernon Kay and the Sugar Babes designed to encourage school children to take a stand against bullying. It also ran a national anti-bullying poetry competition, inviting children to compose a poem that illustrated how bullying was not tolerated in their community.

ChildLine

> ChildLine aims to influence public policy and to change attitudes and practices that affect children's safety and welfare.
>
> (ChildLine website)

Childline is a free, confidential helpline for young people

ChildLine is a free, confidential, 24-hour helpline for children and young people, which offers the guidance and support of trained counsellors to help resolve a whole range of problems. In 2003, ChildLine received 31,000 calls from children and, since it was launched in 1986, the organisation has given counselling to over 1 million people. It offers help in a range of ways, including giving the following advice to the victims of bullying.

- Do not ignore bullying.
- Talk to someone you trust, such as a parent or teacher.
- Keep a record of events.
- Do not retaliate.
- Remember that bullying is not your fault — no one deserves to be bullied.

ChildLine has recently set up ChildLine in Partnership with Schools (CHIPS), a scheme offering practical advice to pupils, teachers and parents.

In recent years, the government has required all schools to develop their own anti-bullying policies and has set up a website that offers guidance and advice both to schools and to pupils. ChildLine has issued a number of guidelines to schools, which it believes will help to solve the problem of bullying:

- Get everyone in the school to help to solve the problem of bullying — children, teachers, playground assistants, dinner staff and others.
- Put anti-bullying posters around the school and books in the library.
- Use school assemblies to explain about the problems of bullying.
- Make sure there are plenty of staff around at breaks and lunchtime, when most bullying happens.

3

- Set up peer counselling schemes — these are groups of older pupils who give advice to younger ones. It is felt that children are better able to explain the problems of bullying than teachers.

Kidscape

Kidscape is an organisation that campaigns for children's safety. It was founded in 1984 by Dr Michele Elliott and its aim is to teach children about personal safety and how to deal with bullying and other difficult situations. Kidscape tries to help children to be safe before the harm occurs.

More than 2 million British school children have been involved in Kidscape's Child Protection Programme, and 16,000 have been helped through the anti-bullying helpline. Kidscape offers support in a variety of ways, including:
- helplines
- posters, books and videos
- national safety training programmes
- confidence-building sessions to help the victims of bullying

In 2000, the *Charity Times UK* gave Kidscape its Charity of the Year Award.

Conflict between families and friends

Perhaps the most common area of conflict in people's everyday lives is within their families or with their friends. There are many reasons for such conflict, for example:
- parents splitting up and getting divorced
- problems over money
- arguments between parents and children over their choice of friends
- conflict over moral issues, such as abortion, cohabitation and parents disagreeing with their grown-up child's choice of partner
- children trying to push their friends into doing something they do not want to do, such as smoking or taking drugs
- rivalry between brothers and sisters

Rivalry between brothers and sisters is a common reason for conflict

All religions are concerned about relationships between family members, which should be based on mutual love, respect and responsibility. Within Christianity, children are called to 'honour your father and your mother' (Exodus 20:12), but parents too are called not to 'provoke your children to anger' (Ephesians 6:4).

Islam teaches that no child should cause harm to the parent and, similarly, parents should cause the child no harm either. Muslims are called to obey their parents even in adulthood, and to accept the authority their wisdom and experience grants them. This may not be easy to do, especially for Muslims who live in a Western culture. Parents have the right to expect obedience from their children, partly in return for what they have done for them. However, if parents demand that children do what is wrong, disobedience becomes not only justifiable but also imperative.

> If you fear a breach between the two, appoint an arbitrator from his people and an arbitrator from her people. If they both want to set things right, Allah will bring about reconciliation between them. Allah knows all, is well aware of everything.
>
> (Surah 4:35)

In Islam, resolving family conflict should first take place within the family, using mediators from within the family who should work together to resolve the conflict, although the husband and wife are not obliged to take their advice. To avoid conflict with friends and fellow Muslims, Islam encourages its followers to avoid gossip, backbiting and fault-finding:

> Beware of suspicion…do not search for faults in each other, do not spy on each other, nor yearn after that which others possess, nor envy, nor entertain malice…but be servants of Allah, brothers and sisters to one another as you have been ordered.
>
> (Muslim, Malik)

Division and conflict between Muslims is a cause of distress to the Muslim community since the Ummah of Islam should be united: 'Believers are one single brotherhood, so make peace and reconciliation between two contenders, and fear Allah, that you may receive mercy' (Surah 49:10). The ideal, taught by the Prophet Muhammad, is always to seek unity and to avoid sectarianism and division: 'Avoid the branching paths, and keep to the general community' (Hadith).

Every week in the newspapers there are stories of conflict, including disputes about money won in the lottery and arguments between neighbours over noisy parties, untidy hedges and high trees. Sometimes such conflicts can result in a family splitting up and friends never speaking to each other again. Conflict is unavoidable and sometimes healthy — it is often the means by which we move on and make important changes in our lives — but excessive conflict, and conflict that causes pain and injury, is unhealthy. Religious believers often feel called to act as peacemakers in situations where conflict exists.

Forgiveness and reconciliation in Christianity

Religions teach that people should look to offer forgiveness to those with whom they have had an argument or come into conflict. Reconciliation is seen as the best way to solve problems between family and friends. Forgiveness means treating the other person as if the conflict, or the reason for conflict, had never occurred. Reconciliation means restoring the relationship to what it was before the dispute occurred.

> Then Peter came to Jesus and asked, 'Lord, how many times shall I forgive my brother when he sins against me? Up to seven times?' Jesus answered, 'I tell you, not seven times, but seventy-seven times.'
> (Matthew 18:21–22)

> And when you stand praying, if you hold anything against anyone, forgive him, so that your Father in heaven may forgive you your sins.
> (Mark 11:25–26)

> Forgiveness is the fundamental condition of the reconciliation of the children of God with their Father and of men with one another.
> (Catechism of the Catholic Church)

Forgiveness depends on a recognition that there has been a real decision to change behaviour on the part of everyone concerned and is based on three requirements:

- an attitude of unconditional love
- dealing with pain, anger and rejection
- facing the future positively

The model of Christian forgiveness is, of course, the forgiveness of God, offered to humans through the death of Jesus. Although humans cannot express the full scope of this divine love and forgiveness, with God's help they can aim to do so, knowing that God will give them grace to forgive those they could not forgive on their own.

Islamic views on forgiveness and reconciliation

Muslims believe they should be forgiving to those whom they have been in conflict with and God is referred to as 'Allah, the Compassionate and Merciful'. The Qur'an teaches that:

- Muslims should be compassionate, reconciling and merciful to others, just as God is compassionate and merciful.
- On the Day of Judgement, God will show mercy and forgiveness to those who have shown mercy and forgiveness to their fellow beings:

> If a person forgives and makes reconciliation, his reward is due from God.
>
> (Surah 42:40)

The Prophet Muhammad taught that people should forgive and be reconciled with those who have offended them.

> Be forgiving and control yourself in the face of provocation; give justice to the person who was unfair and unjust to you.
>
> (Hadith)

However, there are some situations a Muslim would find difficult to resolve, such as those that involve people who work actively against Islam, and those who deny Muslim principles. For this reason, Muslims are warned to avoid associating with those who may influence them away from Islam:

> On that day, the wrongdoer will bite at his hands and say: 'O that I had taken the straight path! Woe is me! Would that I had never taken such a one for a friend. He led me astray.'
>
> (Surah 25:27–30)

Muslims should aim to be sympathetic, unselfish and genuine in their concern for each other:

> Don't sever ties of kinship, don't bear enmity against one another, don't nurse aversion for one another, and don't feel envy against the other. Live as fellow brothers and sisters, as Allah has commanded you.
>
> (Hadith)

Questions and activities

Sample questions and answers

1 Name two weapons of mass destruction. (2 marks)

Nuclear weapons, such as atomic bombs, and biological weapons, such as anthrax, are weapons of mass destruction as they are used to kill vast numbers of people, civilians as well as combatants, at one time.

2 Outline the reasons why some Christians are pacifists. (6 marks)

Some Christians are pacifists — they refuse to fight in war — because they believe violence is always wrong and can never be the right way to resolve conflicts. They use evidence from the Bible to support their claims. For example, the Ten Commandments forbid killing: 'You shall not commit murder' (Exodus 20:13) and a pacifist believes killing in war is no more justified than killing under other circumstances. Jesus taught that people should love their enemies and stopped his own followers from using violence. When Peter drew a sword to fight, Jesus said: 'Put your sword back in its place…for all who draw the sword will die by the sword' (Matthew 26:52). Christian pacifists may argue that if people act peacefully towards each other, then, eventually, peace will be established everywhere, and so it is their responsibility to stand up for peaceful ways of resolving conflict. Nuclear weapons and weapons of mass destruction can cause unimaginable suffering and can never be a justifiable way of dealing with conflict, and so some Christians who may accept that traditional wars are sometimes necessary would still argue for nuclear pacifism.

3 Explain why forgiveness is important for one religion other than Christianity. (8 marks)

Forgiveness is vital within Islam because Allah himself is compassionate and merciful. The Qur'an teaches that Muslims should therefore be compassionate, reconciling and merciful to their friends, family and community members, especially those with whom they have been in conflict. Forgiveness is also vital because it is the only way the Ummah can remain united and be protected against forces which may seek to break it up. Furthermore, on the Day of Judgement Allah will show mercy and forgiveness to Muslims who have shown mercy and forgiveness to their fellow human beings: 'If a person forgives and makes reconciliation, his reward is due from God' (Surah 42:40). Muslims should be sympathetic, unselfish and genuine towards each other and not withhold forgiveness: 'Don't sever ties of kinship, don't bear enmity against one another, don't nurse aversion for one another, and don't feel envy against the other. Live as fellow brothers and sisters, as Allah has commanded you' (Hadith). True forgiveness must therefore mean treating the other person as if the conflict had never taken place and restoring the relationship to what it was before the conflict.

4 'It is easier to resolve conflicts in a religious family than in a non-religious family.' Do you agree? Give reasons for your opinion, showing you have considered another point of view. In your answer, you should refer to religion. (4 marks)

To some extent, this is true, since a religious family should, in theory, have fewer conflicts if they are in agreement over the important matters on which their family life is based. Some of the major reasons for conflict in families — such as divorce, debt, friends, partners, rivalry between brothers and sisters and moral problems like drugs, smoking or school behaviour — might be less of a problem in a religious family because there are often religious rules and teachings that offer strong guidelines in the first place and family members are concerned about following these guidelines out of respect for their religion. When conflict does arise, the principles of forgiveness and reconciliation that are at the heart of religious teaching can be remembered and applied more easily by a family which is determined not to let conflict split them up. They may use biblical or Qur'anic teaching to support them. The New Testament teaches Christian children and parents to live together in love, respect and honour, and Muslim teaching makes it clear that children should obey their parents, even in adulthood, unless they are being encouraged to do something immoral or against Islam.

However, religious people are human too, and there will be times when conflict is not easy to resolve because they will face situations they have never dealt with before and this may be a challenge to them. A strict Muslim father may find it difficult to deal with the conflict that would arise from his daughter going out with a non-Muslim boy, and possibly going to parties where there is alcohol. This would be a stronger conflict than for a non-religious family, and not easy to resolve. Also, we cannot assume that non-religious families are not concerned to resolve conflicts. Even without religious teaching, there are good reasons to live in harmony in a family, and a non-religious family is just as likely to work hard at doing so.

I believe that although religious families may have strong reasons to stay together, non-religious families are going to be just as concerned to be united. In fact, if religious families stay together *only* because they are religious, then this is not as good as non-religious families choosing to stay together.

Further questions

1 Name two areas in the world in which there is conflict. (2 marks)
2 Give an outline of the views of one religion other than Christianity on war. (6 marks)
3 Explain the teaching of Christianity on bullying. (8 marks)
4 'Governments can never justify spending money on stockpiling weapons.' Do you agree? Give reasons for your opinion, showing you have considered another point of view. In your answer, you should refer to religion. (4 marks)

Class activities and homework

Understanding war and peace issues

Your teacher will divide the class into two groups and ask each to use the internet to put together a collage of news and opinion items on a major world conflict of the twentieth or twenty-first century. Decide whether the conflict fulfils the criteria of the just war theory. Under your teacher's guidance, present your findings to the rest of the class.

'Religious people should work for peace at all costs.' Examine this statement in detail, and develop arguments for and against the claim using all the material you have studied.

Understanding conflict between friends and family

In small groups, devise a short role-play to illustrate the problems of bullying at school or in the community. One character in your role-play should be a religious believer. End the role-play with a problem that you want the rest of the class to solve using religious and non-religious teachings. Under your teacher's guidance, present your role-play to the rest of the class.

Explain the main causes of conflict between friends and family and explain how religious teaching can help them to be resolved.

Understanding forgiveness and reconciliation

Your teacher will divide the class into pairs and give each pair a conflict scenario, for example a teenage daughter who has started seeing an older boy and has dropped out of school. In pairs, discuss how the family might resolve the conflict and seek reconciliation. Under your teacher's guidance, present your findings to the rest of the class.

'Forgiving friends is the most important lesson we should learn.' Do you agree? Give reasons for your opinion, showing you have considered another point of view. In your answer, you should refer to religion.

Religion: crime and punishment

The nature of law and justice

The law consists of the rules that govern human relationships and guide people as to how they should behave towards each other in a civilised society. In a country's legal system, laws are made and enforced by the state to enable people living together in society to live in freedom, safety and order. Laws protect the weak from being oppressed by the strong and enable everyone to live in a peaceful situation. Without motoring laws, for example, there would be no control on speed limits and the result would be more accidents and chaos on the roads. Similarly, without other laws, people could kill each other and steal other people's possessions without fear of being punished.

If humans are to live together peacefully in society, laws are needed so that:

- people know how to act towards each other
- people can work and interact with each other without fear
- people are protected from violence and oppression

A system of justice operates alongside the law. Justice is about enforcing laws in a way that is fair and equal for everyone. It is concerned with making sure that the good are rewarded and the evil punished. Without justice, the law could not operate with authority because people would believe it was unfair and society could not function in an orderly way. Therefore, laws are made by the state and justice is enforced through the courts.

Of course, it is not as straightforward as this. Not all human actions are controlled and regulated by the law. For example, there are actions that some people consider to be wrong but which are not against the law, like not washing or being untidy.

The police have a responsibility to maintain order

One particularly important branch of the legal system is criminal law. A **crime** is an action that is against the law and which is forbidden by the state and liable to **punishment**. Certain actions — such as murder, theft and assault — are forbidden and the state, in the form of the police and the courts, will punish anyone who breaks the law through imprisonment or a fine.

However, there are other kinds of wrongdoing. A sin is an act that goes against the will of God. A crime may be a sin as well, but not all sins are crimes. For example, the act of murder is a crime in English law and it is also a sin because it goes against the will of God, according to the Ten Commandments. In contrast, adultery is not a crime in English law, but it is a sin according to most religions. If a law is against the will of God — such as the apartheid laws in South Africa that allowed people to discriminate against other races — religious believers campaign against it. Famous leaders such as Martin Luther King Jr and Nelson Mandela fought against laws that were contrary to the will of God.

Justice is about ensuring that the law is applied fairly to everyone and that rewards and punishments for actions are appropriately given. Thomas Aquinas claimed that law and justice go together, and that if a law is not a just law, people will not follow it. If a government issues unjust laws, people will rebel against them. In the early 1990s, the UK government issued a law requiring people to pay a community charge called the poll tax. Some people thought the law was unfair and there were protests and riots. Eventually, the government withdrew the law. More recently, pro-hunt protestors campaigned against the government's plans to make fox-hunting illegal and succeeded in delaying the final ban on hunting with dogs.

Pro-hunt protestors campaigning against the government's plans to make fox-hunting illegal

How are laws made in the UK?

Laws are made by parliament through a complex procedure. First, the proposed law is written in a document called a bill, which is introduced and debated in the House of Commons. It is then passed to a committee, which goes through the bill in detail before it is debated again. Then a vote is taken, and if the vote is in favour of the bill, it is passed to the House of Lords for discussion. If the House of Lords passes the bill, it is sent to the queen, who gives it the royal assent. The bill then becomes an act of parliament and is law.

In his famous book, *Leviathan*, Thomas Hobbes said that without law, life would be 'solitary, poor, nasty, brutish and short'.

Christian attitudes towards justice

But let justice roll on like a river, righteousness like a never-failing stream!

(Amos 5:24)

Be merciful, just as your Father is merciful.　　(Luke 6:36)

The Bible speaks of God as a just, or righteous, God, who wants humans to live together in justice, peace and fairness. Jesus taught about the need for people to act in a just way towards each other, and Christians should try to make the world a place in which justice prevails. Many Christians have worked to help the poor and the oppressed and to gain a fairer share of the world's resources for everyone: 'Blessed are those who hunger and thirst for righteousness, for they will be filled' (Matthew 5:6).

Christians believe the world should be a just place and that God will reward those who are good and punish those who do evil. The Bible teaches that:

- God is a just God.
- People should be treated fairly and not cheated.
- The rich should share with the poor.
- People should be treated equally.

Islamic attitudes towards justice

O ye who believe! Stand out firmly for justice, as witnesses to God, even though it be against yourselves, your parents or your kindred, whether the case be of a rich person or a poor person.

(Surah 4:135)

The Qur'an teaches that God is just and that he will reward those who are good and punish those who are evil on the Day of Judgement. Muslims believe in the importance of justice because:

- The Qur'an teaches that God wants people to act in justice and fairness to each other.
- Everyone is equal under Islamic law and no citizen should be beneath the protection of the law or above its demands.
- Justice is the basis of the pillar of Zakah.
- The Shari'ah requires justice for everyone.
- Muhammad acted with justice.
- A corrupt society should be challenged and changed.

Muslims believe their duty to God requires them to act justly in their dealings with others and to ensure that society is governed in a fair and just way. This is done by following the law of God, the Shari'ah. Shari'ah Law requires that judges should not try cases when they are angry, hungry or distracted, and the law should be carried out publicly so that justice can be seen to have been done. Protection of the innocent is important, however, and trials and punishments carried out in secret are always wrong. Muslims believe that the law of the land should be the law of God; hence, Islamic justice and the court system have strict rules of fairness.

> All stand equal in the eye of the Islamic law of justice.
> (Nisar Ahmed, *The Fundamental Teachings of the Qur'an and Hadith*)

It is often thought in the West that Islamic justice is harsh, but this is against the principles of Islam. Some cultural aspects of justice have been misunderstood as being Islamic, or are representative of a particularly extreme form of Islam which is not Sunnah (of the prophet). Furthermore, in a society that truly lives by Islamic law, there would be virtually no crimes to warrant the harsh penalties which people in the West often think are characteristic of Islam as a whole. Ultimately, the biggest deterrent in a Muslim society is not the Shari'ah Law but the knowledge that Allah is watching everything they do and every deed is recorded in preparation for the Day of Judgement.

True Islamic justice is not the hunting down of wrongdoers but the desire to establish peace, order and goodness. Muslims must unite to remove wrong and to put it right, not turning a blind eye to injustice. However, what Allah desires most of all is forgiveness and reconciliation: 'The reward for an injury is an equal injury back; but if a person forgives instead and is reconciled, that will earn reward from Allah' (Surah 42:40). If compensation is not made to those who have been wronged in this life, Allah will give it after death. Similarly, if someone suffers wrong judgement in this life, their accuser will pay for it on the Day of Judgement.

Since all people are deemed to have equal rights before the law, Islamic principles work against injustice. For example, Muslims do not charge interest on loans because this takes money from the poor and gives it to the rich. Muslim groups, such as Muslim Aid and Islamic Relief, follow the pillar of Zakah and work to help the poor and bring justice to the world.

> Zakah creates love and brotherhood between rich and poor, it minimises social tension and bridges the gap between them and it provides social and economic security for the whole society.
> (Islamic Relief)

Muslim Aid is an organisation that works to relieve poverty around the world and seeks to secure justice for the poor and oppressed. It provides short-term and long-term aid, together with education and training programmes. It has campaigned hard, asking the rich nations to be more generous in their giving to the poor, and has sought to get rid of oppression in areas of great poverty and deprivation.

Punishment

Theories of punishment

Laws are considered to be most effective when punishment is used to enforce them. Punishments are given to make sure that laws are obeyed and there is justice. The law is enforced by the police force and the court system, and punishments are given to those people who are caught breaking the law. If there were no punishments, it has been argued, not everyone would obey the law and society would lose its sense of order, freedom and justice. In the UK, the main forms of punishment are imprisonment, fines and community service orders. These vary depending on the severity of the crime.

The courts ensure the law is enforced

Minor crimes are dealt with by magistrates' courts, while major ones are dealt with in the crown court. A system of appeals exists and a case can be heard before a higher court — the highest in England is the House of Lords. It is also possible to take a case to the European Court of Justice and the European Court of Human Rights.

However, punishment is not just concerned with making sure everyone obeys the law. There are several purposes behind punishment, including deterrence, retribution, reform and protection.

Deterrence

Deterrence involves preventing or discouraging people from doing something. A punishment given to someone can act as a deterrent to others to prevent them from committing the same crime, or to deter the offender from re-offending. For example, people may be deterred from killing another person if they know that murderers are put in prison for a very long time. If prison is seen as a harsh place, people will be frightened of breaking the law and being sent there.

Retribution

Many feel that those who do wrong ought to suffer as a punishment for what they have done — they should, in some way, pay for their crime. This gives society, and the victims of crime, a feeling of revenge and **retribution**. Moreover, the severity of the punishment should fit the crime — the worse the crime, the harsher the punishment. Thus a person committing a murder will be given a harsher sentence than someone stealing sweets from a shop.

Reform

Punishment should also help to **reform** offenders — this means helping them to see what they have done wrong and ensuring they do not do it again. Reformative punishments include helping prisoners to gain useful qualifications and skills so they can become law-abiding citizens again.

Protection

Many people are frightened by violent criminals. One of the purposes of punishment is to protect ordinary members of society from such offenders by keeping them locked in prison where they can do no harm.

4

Key words

Deterrence
Making punishments so severe that people will be put off (deterred) from committing crimes

Reform
Using punishment to help people not to offend again and helping them to become law-abiding members of society

Retribution
Using punishment to make criminals suffer and pay for the wrong they have done

Prison sentences may serve several functions

Summary

Most punishments include a mixture of all of these factors. For example, putting an offender in prison serves the purposes of deterrence, retribution and protection and, with the aid of education and counselling while in prison, offenders can be reformed. However, the sad reality is that in the UK nearly half of all prisoners commit crime after they are released and they therefore end up being sent back to prison again.

Christian teaching on judgement, forgiveness and punishment

Most Christians support the view that people should obey the law, and that fair and just punishments may be used to protect society and deter people from committing crimes.

Judgement

Key word

Judgement
The act of weighing up and assessing what people have done and what punishments, if any, should be enforced

The Bible teaches that God is just and that he will make his **judgement** on everyone, rewarding those who are good and punishing those who are bad — not necessarily in this life, but in the life to come: 'each person was judged according to what he had done' (Revelation 20:13). However, some Christians see this as a simplistic interpretation of the Bible because it suggests that people can be saved from condemnation by their works. Many Christians claim that the only criterion for judgement is whether a person has accepted Jesus as Lord and Saviour and trusts only in him for salvation. This is the only just way in which God can make a judgement, since no human being could ever be good enough to get to heaven and to be in a relationship with God. God therefore offers one way to salvation that is open to everyone, irrespective of what they have done or what kind of people they are. The decision is a vital one as it determines life over death, heaven over hell, but it is the fairest means on which God can base his judgement.

Judgement is not viewed in a negative way — it is seen as bringing the consequences of someone's actions into the open. Jesus himself said there would be a judgement on all people and that God would be the final judge: 'You judge by human standards: I pass judgement on no one. But if I do judge, my decisions are right, because I am not alone, I stand with the

Father, who sent me' (John 8:15–16). Jesus taught that it was not for humans to make judgement, but for God. He said that the most important thing was to show forgiveness to those who had done wrong: 'Do not judge, and you will not be judged. Do not condemn, and you will not be condemned. Forgive, and you will be forgiven' (Luke 6:37).

Forgiveness

Christianity is based on the concepts of love and forgiveness. The Bible teaches that humanity is cut off from God because of sin, but that God, through his love for all people, sent his son Jesus to allow Christians to be forgiven their sins and to have their relationship with God restored.

> For God so loved the world that he gave his one and only Son, that whoever believes in him shall not perish but have eternal life. For God did not send his Son into the world to condemn the world, but to save the world through him.
>
> (John 3:16–17)

The Bible teaches that:

- It is possible for people to change their ways and that people should be able to call upon the help of God to change their lives.
- Jesus died to bring forgiveness and reconciliation.
- Christians should not judge other people.
- Christians should be forgiving.
- Christians should settle their problems without the use of courts.
- Christians should obey the authorities.

> Why do you look at the speck of sawdust in your brother's eye and pay no attention to the plank in your own eye?
>
> (Luke 6:41)

Christians believe that forgiveness will be offered by God to anyone who is truly sorry for what they have done and who seriously wants to change the way they live — this is what the Bible calls repentance. This can be done through prayer and, in the Catholic Church, by confession before a priest, followed by what are known as acts of contrition and penance. The Lord's Prayer includes this important concept: 'Forgive us our sins, as we forgive those who sin against us' (Luke 11:4).

Punishment

Christianity teaches that the proper purpose of punishment is to reform prisoners and help them return to society as law-abiding citizens. Many Christians have worked hard trying to ensure prisoners are treated properly, and many prison reforms have been made after campaigns by Christians.

Elizabeth Fry campaigned for improved living conditions in prisons

One such Christian reformer was the Quaker, Elizabeth Fry (1780–1845), who visited Newgate Prison and tried to help the women and children held as prisoners there, who were living in dreadful conditions. She found over 300 women prisoners with their children, huddled together in two wards, and cells without clean clothes or bedding and very little food. She started a campaign to improve sanitation and living conditions and ensured all prisoners had decent clothing and food. She also established a school for the children, a prison chapel and proper supervision of the prisoners by trained matrons and monitors. In a letter to her daughter in 1813, Elizabeth Fry wrote:

> I have lately been to Newgate to see after the poor prisoners who had poor little infants without clothing or with very little and I think if you saw how small a piece of bread they are each allowed a day you would be very sad.

The Christian Churches have always supported the notion of punishment, so long as it is fair and just. In the Middle Ages, cathedrals offered sanctuary and protection to criminals who sought shelter in them and, in recent times, Churches have campaigned for society to use fair and just laws and punishments to protect society and reform criminals. Today, there is a growing body of opinion within the Christian Church that more emphasis should be placed on helping prisoners to reform rather than just locking them up.

The United Reformed Church believes that even the most depraved person is capable of reform and that it is society's role to offer that possibility of reform through the systems of confinement and imprisonment which the state organises.

(United Reformed Church statement)

Today, Quakers are deeply concerned for those who are involved with crime and are 'punished' by our present system.... Experience in prison can badly damage people and it rarely stops crime. Prison is punishment not only for offenders but also for their families.... Quakers would like to see a more positive approach taken towards everyone involved with crime and punishment.

(Quaker statement)

These views support the teaching of Jesus, who said: 'I needed clothes and you clothed me, I was sick and you looked after me, I was in prison and you came to visit me...I tell you the truth, whatever you did for one of the least of these brothers of mine, you did for me' (Matthew 25:36,40).

Islamic teaching on judgement, forgiveness and punishment

Be forgiving and control yourself in the face of provocation; give justice to the person who was unfair and unjust to you; give to someone even though he did not give to you when you were in need, and keep fellowship with the one who did not reciprocate your concern.

(Hadith)

Islam teaches that Allah is merciful and that those who are sorry for the wrongs they have done will be forgiven. In the same way, Muslims should forgive those who have wronged them: 'If anyone does evil or wrongs his own soul, but afterwards seeks God's forgiveness, he will find God Oft-forgiving, Most Merciful' (Surah 4:110). Muslims believe that to commit a crime is a sin against God, and that on the Day of Judgement God will punish sins. Muslims use punishment as a deterrent and to reform prisoners.

Islamic attitudes towards punishment are governed by the following principles:

- The Qur'an lays down the punishments that should be given for certain crimes. For example, the amputation of limbs: 'As to the thief, male or female, cut off his or her hands: a punishment by way of example, from God, for their crime' (Surah 5:41). Whipping and amputation allow the offender to stay within society and with their family, and the severity of the punishment is seen by other people and will deter them from crime.
- However, strict punishments such as these are only given as a last resort and the offender's background and family circumstances are always taken into account — a person would not have their hand amputated, for example, if they stole to feed a starving baby.

> The recompense for an injury is an injury equal thereto in degree: but if a person forgives and makes retribution, his reward is due from God; for God loves not those who do wrong.
>
> (Surah 42:40)

In Muslim society, anti-social and dangerous criminals are imprisoned to protect citizens. It is also possible, under Islamic law, for a criminal to be made to pay compensation to the victim of their crime, or to the victim's family, as a form of retribution.

Prisoners of conscience

> Blessed are those who are persecuted because of righteousness, for theirs is the kingdom of heaven.
>
> (Matthew 5:10)

A prisoner of conscience is someone who has been imprisoned because they have followed their religious beliefs and, in doing so, have offended the government of the nation they are living in. Amnesty International defines prisoners of conscience as:

> Persons detained by reason of their political, religious or other conscientiously held beliefs, or by reason of their ethnic origin, sex, colour, language, national or social origin, economic status, birth or other status, provided they have not used or advocated violence.

Amnesty International is a worldwide movement of people campaigning for human rights. It works on behalf of prisoners of conscience throughout the world and seeks to establish fair trials and justice for all political prisoners and the abolition of the death penalty.

Amnesty International's vision is of a world where every person enjoys all of the human rights established in the Universal Declaration of Human Rights and other international human rights standards.

(Amnesty International website)

Dietrich Bonhoeffer

One of the most famous prisoners of conscience was Dietrich Bonhoeffer (1906–45), a German Christian who was imprisoned and executed for his religious beliefs by the Nazis in the Second World War.

Dietrich Bonhoeffer

Bonhoeffer had seen the horrors of the First World War and the suffering had convinced him that war was wrong, so he became a Christian pacifist. He studied theology at university and later became a lecturer and chaplain at Berlin University. He was alarmed by the rise of the Nazi Party in Germany and opposed its policies. In 1933, he openly broadcast and criticised Hitler and the Nazis about their treatment of the Jews. He said of Hitler: 'The leader who makes an idol of himself and his office makes a mockery of God' (Bonhoeffer's 1933 radio broadcast).

Angered by his attack, the Nazis banned Bonhoeffer from teaching in Berlin and he was forced to move to London, where he became a pastor at two German churches. During this time, he began to meet with important British Church leaders to tell them what the Nazis were doing.

In 1935, he went back to Germany and became the head of a college that trained student pastors who opposed the Nazis. Bonhoeffer continued to preach sermons claiming that Christians should not obey any Nazi laws that were contrary to the teachings of Jesus, and he taught his students that their Christian principles meant they should oppose the Nazis. Moreover, he communicated with Church leaders all over the world and told them not to have any dealings with the Protestant Church in Germany because it was controlled by the Nazis. He also contacted the Jewish leader, Martin

Niemöller, and tried to help the Jews in Germany. The Nazis were enraged by all this and Bonhoeffer was arrested in 1937 and his college shut down. He was released a few weeks later and exiled from Berlin.

Although he was a pacifist, Bonhoeffer realised that peaceful protest was not going to work against the Nazis. He believed that, as a Christian, he should oppose the evil of the Nazis and he became involved with a group of German army officers in a series of plots to assassinate Hitler.

When war broke out, Bonhoeffer went to the USA, but he soon returned to Germany. He believed that, if he was to be an effective minister when the conflict was over, it was important to suffer alongside his people. In 1943, he was arrested for undermining the German armed forces. During his time in prison, he wrote one of his most famous works, *Letters and Papers from Prison*, in which he condemned the evil and suffering of war. In this book, he wrote about the problems of injustice:

> It is the advantage and the nature of the strong that they can bring crucial issues to the fore and take a clear position regarding them. The weak always have to choose between alternatives that are not their own.

In July 1944, an attempt to assassinate Hitler by exploding a bomb near him failed. The Nazis investigated and found out that Bonhoeffer had been one of the conspirators. He was taken to Buchenwald concentration camp and then on to Flossenburg extermination camp, where he was executed in April 1945.

Nelson Mandela

Nelson Mandela

In more recent times, perhaps the most famous prisoner of conscience has been Nelson Mandela (born 1918). As a young man, he joined the African National Congress (ANC), an organisation that campaigned against racial discrimination and the system of apartheid government in South Africa. Apartheid gave power to white people and oppressed the black majority, who lived in poor conditions and worked for little money. Black workers were exploited and many of the towns and villages they lived in had little sanitation and limited access to decent schools and hospitals.

Mandela advocated peaceful protest, but he was continually harassed by the South African government and police. In 1956, he was charged with high treason, though the charges were later dropped. In 1960, 69 black protesters were shot by the authorities while protesting peacefully, in what became known as the Sharpeville Massacre. In response to this, Mandela, now vice president of the ANC, led a campaign against racial oppression. He was arrested by the South African government and charged with sabotage and attempting to overthrow the government.

In 1984, Nelson Mandela was sentenced to life imprisonment. Meanwhile, protests continued throughout South Africa and eventually the nations of the world took notice. International sanctions were imposed on the South African government in 1987.

After many years, the protests finally paid off and the system of apartheid was ended. In 1990, Mandela was released from prison and set to work alongside the new South African President F. W. de Klerk to establish peace and justice in South Africa. The two men were awarded the Nobel peace prize in 1993, and the following year Nelson Mandela was elected President of South Africa. He retired in 1999.

> I have cherished the idea of a democratic and free society in which all persons live together in harmony with equal opportunities. It is an ideal which I hope to live for and to achieve. But if needs be, it is an ideal for which I am prepared to die.
>
> (Nelson Mandela)

Capital punishment

Capital punishment means taking the life of a condemned prisoner. It is called the death penalty and applies only to the most serious offences (capital offences), such as murder.

The death penalty was abolished in the UK in 1965 by the Murder (Abolition of the Death Penalty) Act 1965. The last two people executed were condemned murderers Peter Allen and John Walby, who were hanged on 13 August 1964. Under the European Convention on Human Rights, which Britain signed in 1999,

Key word

Capital punishment
The death penalty

execution was abolished throughout the European Union. Other nations, including the USA, still have the death penalty. It is estimated that there is one legal execution nearly every day, somewhere in the world.

There have been many debates over the years, in the UK and elsewhere, about whether the death penalty is an effective punishment or not, and there are persuasive arguments on both sides.

Non-religious arguments concerning the death penalty

Many people believe murderers and those who commit serious crimes or acts of terrorism should be executed. The reasons for this view are:

The electric chair

- The death penalty acts as a deterrent to those contemplating committing a serious crime.
- The death penalty means that society can rid itself of the most dangerous people, so they cannot be a threat again.
- The value of human life is made clear by executing those who kill others.
- Execution is the ultimate retribution and is compensation for taking the life of another.
- Execution gives the victim's family a sense of retribution.
- Execution is cheaper than keeping a prisoner in prison for life.

Death penalty protestors

However, others argue against the death penalty. The reasons for their views are:
- In countries where the death penalty is enforced, the number of murders does not seem to drop — execution is no deterrent to someone considering a major crime.
- Many people have been executed who, it was later discovered, were innocent.
- Murderers who know they will face the death penalty if caught are more likely to kill people to avoid capture.

- Terrorists who are executed can end up as martyrs and this encourages more terrorism.
- Human life is important and should not be taken away under any circumstances.
- Murderers do not expect to be caught.
- Murderers often feel execution is an easier punishment than life imprisonment.

Capital punishment and Christianity

The Bible does not give a clear teaching on the question of the death penalty and Christians have differing views. Christians who believe that the death penalty is wrong argue that:

- Christianity is based on the teachings and example of Jesus, who came to reform and save wrongdoers — an executed criminal cannot be reformed.
- Jesus and the apostle Paul taught that retribution is wrong. 'Do not repay anyone evil for evil. Be careful to do what is right in the eyes of everybody' (Romans 12:17).
- Christians believe human life is sacred and a gift from God, and that only God has the right to take life.
- Most Christian Churches are against capital punishment.

However, some Christians believe the death penalty may be used as a way of preventing serious crime and keeping order in society. They argue that:

- The Old Testament allowed capital punishment.
- In the Middle Ages, the Christian Church used capital punishment against those who challenged the authority of the Church.
- Some famous Christians, such as St Thomas Aquinas, have argued that maintaining peace and order in society is more important than reforming a wrongdoer.

Capital punishment and Islam

> Take not life — which God has made sacred — except for just cause.
>
> (Surah 17:33)

The Qur'an teaches that capital punishment may be applied in just causes. Islamic law, the Shari'ah, has taken this teaching to mean permitting the death penalty for three offences: murder, adultery and apostasy (where a Muslim denies Islam and works against it, which is similar to an act of treason). However, before the death penalty is given, the crime must be clearly proven by proper legal processes.

> The shedding of the blood of a Muslim is not lawful except for three reasons: a life for a life, a married person who commits adultery and one who turns aside from his religion and abandons the community.
>
> (Hadith)

When the Prophet Muhammad was ruler of Madinah, it was said that he sentenced people to death for murder and made several statements agreeing with the death penalty. However, there are many Muslims who do not feel capital punishment is right. They argue that the Qur'an does not make capital punishment obligatory, only an option.

The Western news media are quick to pick up on cases in which Muslim women are under sentence of death for adultery. Although the death penalty is required for adultery under Shari'ah Law, the circumstances must be carefully assessed. The death penalty applies only to committed, married, free Muslims, and the act has to be committed in public and testified by four witnesses. Any false witnesses would themselves be flogged. Interestingly, there were no such witnessed cases during the Prophet Muhammed's own lifetime.

Questions and activities

Sample questions and answers

1 What is a sin? (2 marks)

A sin is an act against the will of God, for example murder.

2 Outline the life and work of a prisoner of conscience. (6 marks)

Dietrich Bonhoeffer (1906–45) was a German Christian who was imprisoned and executed for his religious beliefs by the Nazis in the Second World War. He was alarmed by the rise of the Nazi Party and opposed its policies, and, in 1933, he criticised Hitler and the Nazis for their treatment of the Jews.

In 1935, he became the head of a college that trained student pastors who opposed the Nazis. Bonhoeffer continued to preach sermons, claiming that Christians should not obey any Nazi laws that were contrary to the teachings of Jesus. He taught his students that their Christian principles meant they should oppose the Nazis. All this enraged the Nazis — Bonhoeffer was arrested in 1937 and his college was shut down. He was released a few weeks later and exiled from Berlin.

In 1943, he was arrested again, this time on the grounds of undermining the German armed forces. During his time in prison, he wrote one of his most famous works *Letters and Papers from Prison*.

In July 1944, an attempt to assassinate Hitler by exploding a bomb near him failed. The Nazis investigated and found out that Bonhoeffer had been one of the conspirators. He was taken to Buchenwald concentration camp and then on to Flossenburg extermination camp, where he was executed in April 1945.

3 Explain the differing attitudes among Christians to capital punishment. (8 marks)

The Bible does not give a clear teaching on the death penalty and Christians have differing views. Christians may argue that it is wrong because Christianity is based on the teachings and example of Jesus, who came to reform and save wrongdoers, and the death penalty takes away the possibility of ever reforming a criminal. The death penalty is also the ultimate form of retribution and both Jesus and Paul taught that retribution is wrong. Paul wrote in Romans 12:17: 'Do not repay anyone evil for evil. Be careful to do what is right in the eyes of everybody.' Christians believe that all life is sacred and a gift from God, which only he has the right to take away. They may argue that the death penalty violates the principle of the sanctity of life and that it is hypocritical for Christians to condemn murder but support the death penalty. As a result, most Christian Churches are opposed to capital punishment.

However, some Christians believe that the death penalty — or the threat of the death penalty — is a good way to prevent serious crime and keep society in order. They use the Old Testament to support their argument, since the death penalty is allowed in the Old Testament as the punishment for many offences. Indeed, in the Middle Ages, the Church itself used capital punishment against those who challenged its authority and some important Christian thinkers, such as Thomas Aquinas, have argued that maintaining order in society is more important than reforming an offender. It is significant that many states in the USA which have a large number of Christians among their population support the death penalty.

4 'It is worse to commit a sin than it is to commit a crime.' Do you agree? Give reasons for your opinion, showing you have considered another point of view. In your answer, you should refer to religion. (4 marks)

A sin is an act against God, whereas a crime is an act against a fellow citizen and the state. Many sins, such as murder and theft, are also crimes. Whether or not committing a crime or a sin is worse depends on which way you look at it. From society's point of view, a crime is worse because it affects other people. Society has to pay for the criminal by providing police, the courts and the prisons. Crime can also lead to innocent people suffering. The person committing the crime may experience it as worse than a sin because they face punishment, which usually involves physical and mental discomfort.

A sin is worse from the perspective of a religious believer because it is an action against the God they are supposed to love, worship and obey. Unlike a crime, a sinful action affects the wrongdoer in a more personal or spiritual way and may have longer lasting consequences. For a non-believer, committing a sin may not matter so much, as they do not believe in God.

Probably the answer lies somewhere in the middle. Committing a crime and committing a sin are both wrong in their own ways, and both should therefore be avoided.

Further questions

1 What does the word 'deterrence' mean? (2 marks)

2 Outline the teaching of Christianity and one other religion on the need for forgiveness. (6 marks)

3 Explain the importance of law and justice in modern society. (8 marks)

4 'Punishment should only be for the purpose of reforming the wrongdoer.' Do you agree? Give reasons for your opinion, showing you have considered another point of view. (4 marks)

Class activities and homework

Understanding crime and sin

In small groups, divide a large sheet of paper into two columns. Label one column 'Crime' and the other 'Sin'. Write as many examples as you can think of in each column, then identify which actions are *both* crimes and sins, and which are *only* crimes or *only* sins. Under your teacher's guidance, present your findings to the rest of the class and consider together why this is so. Try to agree on an answer to the question: Is there a real difference between a sin and a crime?

'Committing a sin should be a crime.' Do you agree? Give reasons for your opinion, showing you have considered other points of view. In your answer, you should refer to religion.

Understanding justice and forgiveness

Your teacher will divide the class into three groups, and give each group one of the three dilemmas outlined below.

1 A husband kills his wife because she is suffering from a painful and incurable disease.

2 A suspected terrorist is imprisoned without trial.

3 A married woman commits adultery.

In relation to the dilemma you have been given, answer the following two questions:

1 How would a religious believer respond?

2 How would you respond?

Under your teacher's guidance, share your views with the rest of the class.

Some people say certain crimes and sins are unforgivable. Can you think of any real-life examples of what these might be? Do you think they are forgivable or not? Give reasons for your answer.

Understanding law making

In pairs or small groups, write down the three laws that the UK already has which you think are the most important, and the three laws you think are the least important. Imagine you are ruler for a day. Which laws would you introduce and which laws would you abolish? As a class, brainstorm to see if there is a common consensus. Discuss why you have come up with the changes you have.

How does parliament make laws in the UK?

Understanding the nature of punishment

In pairs or small groups, look at a newspaper. Find as many articles as you can that are concerned with (a) crimes being committed and (b) punishments. In your group consider whether or not the UK punishes wrongdoers appropriately and whether it is too easy or too harsh on wrongdoers. Consider which punishments you would give to murderers, thieves and terrorists. Under your teacher's guidance, share your views with the rest of the class.

'Religious believers are too soft on wrongdoers.' Do you agree? Give reasons for your opinion, showing you have considered other points of view.

Understanding capital punishment

In pairs or small groups, consider the reasons why capital punishment has been abolished in the UK and Europe. Consider why countries such as the USA and those in the Middle East still have the death penalty. Does capital punishment really work as a punishment and a deterrent? Under your teacher's guidance, share your views with the rest of the class.

What are the arguments for and against capital punishment?
Is capital punishment a good or bad thing and is there a better alternative?

Religion and medical issues

Infertility

For a woman to be infertile means she is unable to conceive a child by the usual natural process. For a man to be infertile means he is unable to produce sperm that have the capacity to fertilise a woman's egg.

Up to 10% of couples in the UK who want to have children suffer from problems of **infertility** and, for many of them, it brings great pain. Some couples may be able to accept that it is God's choice for them not to have children. Others may use their parental skills in other areas of their lives. However, some couples will go to almost any lengths to have a child. Some religious believers consider artificial methods of conception wrong, but others recognise that

Key word

Infertility
Being unable to conceive a child naturally

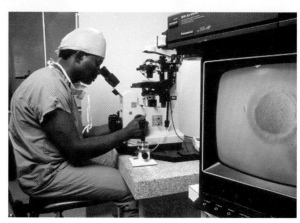

In vitro fertilisation

those who suffer from infertility endure great mental and emotional pain and need to be helped as much as those who have suffered the death of a child. For these people, **fertility treatment** might be a blessing. D. Gareth Jones argues that the use of medical fertility treatment may sometimes 'be pursued for unworthy motives or in a grossly excessive manner' but this is not always the case, and so, in principle, it is not against religious teaching.

Key word

Fertility treatment
Using medical technology to conceive a child

There is a wide range of medical treatments for infertility now available, all of which pose potential problems for religious believers.

- In vitro fertilisation (IVF): in this process, an egg is taken from the mother's womb. It is fertilised in a dish in a laboratory using sperm from her partner or a donor. The resulting embryo is inserted into her womb, where it develops to full term.
- Artificial insemination by husband/partner (AIH): the partner's sperm is medically inserted into the neck of the mother's womb.
- Artificial insemination by donor (AID): the sperm of a donor, usually unknown to the couple, is medically inserted into the neck of the mother's womb.
- Egg donation: the partner's sperm is used to fertilise the egg of an unknown donor female in a dish in a laboratory, and the embryo is inserted into the woman's womb.
- Embryo donation: both sperm and egg are provide by anonymous donors, fertilised in a dish and the embryo is inserted into the woman's womb.
- Surrogacy: another woman carries a baby for an infertile couple. There are two types of surrogacy — traditional or gestational. In traditional surrogacy, the partner's sperm is used to fertilise the egg of the surrogate mother using artificial insemination. In gestational surrogacy, IVF is used to create an embryo using the natural parents' egg and sperm. It is then inserted into the surrogate's womb. In both types of surrogacy, the surrogate carries the baby to full term before handing it over to the couple.

Medical fertility treatments in the UK are currently controlled by the Human Fertilisation and Embryology Authority (HFEA), which exists to ensure that treatments are developed and used ethically. Although some treatments are available on the NHS, not all are, and the methods are expensive. Infertility treatment raises many ethical questions, not just about appropriate use of medical technology but also about human rights. For example, is it legitimate for a woman to be inseminated with her dead husband's frozen sperm, if he has not left specific permission for this? Should women donate their own eggs to help childless couples or to further embryo research? Is it right for men to donate sperm but not to be responsible for the financial maintenance of any children conceived by AID? Should children conceived through the use of donor sperm, eggs, embryos or traditional surrogacy have a right to know their biological parents?

In the UK and overseas, women are paid to donate their eggs, which are in short supply and needed desperately by infertile women who are unable to conceive. The average rate of payment is £150 but this is likely to rise significantly to as much as £1,000 as clinics face a greater demand for fertility treatment than there are donated eggs available. In Romania, where the cost of living is significantly lower, women are also paid £150 for egg donation. Although some claim they donate purely out of concern for infertile women, £150 represents an average month's salary in Romania. Even though everyone seems to benefit, some would still argue that there are ethical problems. Are the donors being exploited? Are they doing something in their own long-term interests? Is it morally right to receive payment for donating part of your body?

Christian attitudes to infertility treatment

Embryology

Christians are divided over the use of infertility treatment, mainly because the methods used result from research carried out on embryos. This research may make use of aborted embryos, embryos formed especially for the purpose of research, or embryos that are the by-product of fertility treatment — unused embryos. There are potential problems in all these cases and Catholics and many other Christians oppose fertility treatment based on embryo research for this reason. Using aborted embryos for research purposes may be seen as bringing some possible future good out of a bad situation, but it may also be argued that such research supports abortion. It is only because abortion is legal that such research can be carried out, but this does not justify abortion.

The creation of embryos specifically for research purposes is even more problematic because it involves making life for the sake of scientific experiments. If life begins at conception — the moment egg and sperm meet — then even a day-old embryo has full human life and all the rights and potential that belong to it. Experimenting on an embryo would then be no better than experimenting on a baby born prematurely at 7 months, a 2-year-old, or even an adult. However, for some Christians, embryos up to the age of 14 days do not possess personhood — that mysterious and difficult-to-determine quality which makes people human beings and makes human life sacred (holy). The Methodist Church, for example, claims that: 'Embryos up to 14 days old can be used for infertility treatments and medical research.'

Using embryos that are not needed for fertility treatment raises the question of 'doomed embryos'. In the course of fertility treatment, a number of successfully fertilised embryos may be produced. Some of these will be

Some Christians argue that medical technology should be used to give couples the opportunity to have children

implanted, others may be frozen for possible use in the future. This raises two possible problems. Usually more than one embryo is implanted to increase the chances of carrying one to full term. If, say, two are lost, and one successfully develops, is there a moral problem concerning the lost two? Were they irresponsibly and immorally fertilised and implanted in the full knowledge that they were likely to be lost? Some would argue that this is the case, although others may claim that the risk is justifiable and not against the sanctity of life. A further problem occurs if the frozen embryos are not used. If they are not implanted, they will be destroyed and, for many Christians, especially Catholics, this is no different from abortion. However, although the loss of the embryo is not accidental, the 'doctrine of double effect' may help. Although the frozen and unused embryos are destroyed, they were not fertilised *in order* to be destroyed at some future date and the loss of some embryos is an unintended result.

Other Christians are prepared to accept IVF despite the problem of **embryology** on the grounds that medical technology should be used to give couples the opportunity to have children — a joy and, some may argue, a right. The principle here is that God gives humans the potential to be able to discover methods of treating infertility. Therefore, infertility treatments are merely an extension of what God has naturally equipped most humans to do.

Key word

Embryology
Medical research using embryos

Non-sexual fertilisation

The use of fertility treatments troubles some Christians, particularly Catholics, on the grounds that in such treatments fertilisation takes place separately from sexual intercourse. Since God intended having children to be the result of sex, having children by any other means is morally wrong. This is a strict view, influenced by Natural Moral Law, which states that what is good is what is natural and anything that moves away from this is questionable.

> Techniques which allow someone other than the husband and wife to be involved in the making of a child are very wrong. Techniques which separate sex from the making of the baby are unacceptable.
>
> (Catechism of the Catholic Church)

This view could be supported by the argument that the sexual relationship between partners is not just physical but emotional, and the conception of a child — the outcome of this relationship — is the richest experience a couple can have. To reduce conception to a scientific process is not what God intended. However, this does not solve the problem of how infertile couples should approach sex. If having children and sex are linked, should an infertile couple have a sexual relationship? Is the emotional bond created by sex available only to those who have the ability to have a child? Such a view would, of course, consider contraception a misuse of the sex act since all acts of sexual intercourse should be open to the possibility of procreation.

For most Christians, the dilemma of infertility is not whether an infertile couple is morally permitted to have a sexual relationship, but whether to consider other means of conceiving. For many, if both sperm and egg are from the husband and wife, there are few problems. Medical technology simply enables them to fertilise in conditions that increase the chance of a successful pregnancy. However, trying to have a child is so emotionally and financially draining that some Christians may argue that wisdom must be used in deciding how long the attempt should go on.

The use of donor sperm or eggs has made it possible for homosexual couples to have children who are related to them

Use of donor sperm or eggs raises other problems. Since most donors remain anonymous, the child may want to find out later in life who their donor parents are. This can cause hurt and unhappiness for everyone involved. Use of donor sperm and eggs has made it increasingly possible for homosexual couples to pursue their wish to have a child who is in some way related to them. This extends the religious and ethical problems further to include the question of whether homosexuals have a right to a child. For those Christians who condemn homosexual acts altogether, the answer is obvious. Since homosexuality is wrong, there is no question of even asking whether a homosexual should have a child. For others, acceptance of the right of an individual to a loving homosexual relationship leads to the question of whether they should have a child — an important goal for many heterosexual couples.

Surrogacy

Surrogacy brings with it the potential for enormous emotional upset. In traditional surrogacy, even though the child is not conceived through an act of sexual intercourse, the father, in some way, forms a bond with the surrogate mother. It could be argued that she becomes a second partner, which breaks the 'one flesh' principle of marriage. Another important issue is that of rights. Whose rights are most important: the surrogate's? the parents'? the child's? Nevertheless, where all other attempts at having a child have failed, surrogacy may seem to be a lifeline to infertile couples, and women who are prepared to bear a child in this way could be seen to be making an extremely generous gesture.

Most Christians are cautious about surrogacy, and many are opposed to it altogether. Interestingly, the case of Abraham, Sarah and Hagar (Genesis 16) gives an example of the dangers of surrogacy. Sarah seems to be unable to conceive despite God's promise to Abraham that he would have an heir. As was culturally acceptable at the time, Sarah suggests to Abraham that he should have a child with her maid, Hagar. Once Ishmael is born to Hagar, the tension between Sarah and Hagar becomes unbearable, and Sarah sends her away from the household, although Hagar is told by God to return. When Sarah herself gives birth to Isaac, the tension rises again. Unable to watch Isaac and Ishmael playing together without fear that Ishmael will inherit what was rightfully Isaac's, Sarah tells Abraham to get rid of Hagar and her son for good. Although these circumstances are unusual, it is interesting that even when Sarah and Abraham thought they were acting for the best, the consequences were not happy for anyone.

Although carefully controlled legal surrogacy may seem to be an ideal solution to the problem of childlessness for many couples, the risks are high. All parties involved need to be certain that the terms they agree to before conception are realistic and that everyone will be able to keep to them after the baby is born. John Stott writes: 'In surrogacy, even if both sperm and ovum are contributed by the married couple, a physical and emotional bonding takes place between the "mother" and the child she is carrying, which may later be hard to break' (*Issues Facing Christians Today*).

Alternatives to infertility treatment

All Christian Churches encourage their members to consider **adoption** as an alternative to infertility treatment. This may also apply to couples who already have a biological family but are in a position to offer a loving adoptive environment to more children. Adoption fulfils many biblical and religious ideals, reflecting the relationships between the Christian and God and between all Christians, who share a family relation-ship under the Fatherhood of God irrespective of their biological family relationships. Adoption expresses the principle of agape — an attitude of genuine Christian love — in action because it reaches out to those in need as well as fulfilling the desires of the couple who long for children.

Key word

Adoption
A legally binding relationship between a couple and a child to whom they are not biologically related

It has become common to adopt children from countries that suffer social, political and economic problems, and many parents now make the deliberate choice to go outside the UK to adopt. Some Christians may feel called by God to adopt or foster children from troubled backgrounds or with serious health or behavioural problems, reflecting the love of Jesus for those who are rejected by society.

Adopting children from overseas is a way of sharing family love with those who have had a troubled start to life.

However, there are problems facing couples who want to adopt. The process of being accepted for adoption is long and demanding. Prospective adoptive parents are expected to face close scrutiny and to pass many tests of suitability, which are never applied to those who conceive naturally or who use fertility treatments. Some couples have gone to extreme lengths to get around these problems, including adopting over the internet or smuggling babies out of war-torn countries. In principle, Christians are opposed to illegal or morally questionable methods of adoption, but some may ask whether it is better to help a child in need even if the law must be stretched to do so.

Adoption raises sensitive issues about the future of the child, most particularly how much contact, if any, they will have with their birth parents. Adopted children can gain access to information about their birth mothers when they reach adulthood, and it is often thought essential for an adopted child's sense of identity to do this, while still recognising the unique relationship that exists between the child and their adoptive parents.

Islamic attitudes to infertility treatment

The pursuit of pregnancy is considered legitimate within Islam and individuals may resort to the necessary means provided they do not violate Shari'ah Law. However, Islam does not allow the use of fertility treatments that deny children the right to know their natural parents. Surrogacy and adoption are banned in Islam, but because the family is so important for Muslims, medical technology can be used to facilitate conception. 'As long as the husband's semen is used, it is permissible for doctors to use artificial means to fertilise the wife's egg' (*Articles of Islamic Acts*, Iman Al-Khoei). Islamic teaching is accepting of IVF and AIH on the grounds that the sperm and egg used come from the husband and wife. According to Islamic belief, the unused embryos are not foetuses because they are less than 14 days old, so their destruction is not the same as abortion. Islam teaches that the soul does not enter the foetus until 120 days, so unused embryos are well within the permissible time.

Because divorce or death bring a marriage contract to an end, a woman may not use the sperm of her former husband that has been kept in a sperm bank. Use of sperm or eggs from any third party is also not permissible as it would be considered an interference with the marriage bond.

Interestingly, Islam offers another response to the problems of infertility in that Muslim men are permitted, under the right conditions, to take up to four wives. Only two of Muhammad's wives had children, and Ayesha, said to be particularly loved by the Prophet, had none. He set the example of how to treat all wives justly and fairly, the fertile as well as the infertile.

Non-religious attitudes to infertility treatment

While it should not be assumed that all non-religious attitudes to infertility treatment are positive, most take the view that it is a good way of using medical technology to help those who are unable to conceive naturally. The claim that everyone has a right to a child is used to support the development of fertility treatment and to increase its availability. However, there is some division over how readily available it should be. For those who can afford private healthcare, multiple attempts at IVF may be possible. For those who rely on the NHS, this is less likely as IVF is extremely expensive and NHS services often have to make difficult decisions about use of resources.

A 56-year-old mother, New York. Should women over natural childbearing age be allowed to conceive through IVF?

Some areas of the UK offer IVF free on the NHS, but others do not, and it has been called a 'postcode lottery' whether someone lives in an area that offers free IVF. For those who believe that infertility treatment is a good thing, there are still reservations about who should benefit from it. For example, should women over natural childbearing age be allowed to conceive through IVF?

The view that it is everyone's right to have a child may also be challenged by evolution. Arguably, natural selection may select a few people to be infertile in order to keep the population numbers down. It is possible too that it is natural for some people to be infertile and for some to be homosexual, so that there are always people able to share the responsibility of childcare within the family. These are controversial arguments, but they may lead to the claim that infertility may, in some cases, be a good thing.

There is no guarantee that fertility treatment will work for everyone, however many attempts they make or how much money they spend. For some couples, coming to terms with childlessness may be their only option.

Genetic engineering

Designer babies

Key word

Genetic engineering
Changing the gene structure, primarily to cure genetically inherited diseases by modifying affected genes

Genetic engineering is a rapidly growing technology that essentially involves changing the gene structure, primarily to cure genetically inherited diseases by modifying affected genes. Although this can be enormously beneficial, there are important moral issues to consider. One of these is that while genetic engineering can be used to cure diseases, it could also, in theory, be used to add desirable characteristics such as intelligence, physical attractiveness or gender. It could get rid of characteristics such as baldness, addictions or short-sightedness, for example.

For Christians, genetic engineering is against the spirit of Psalm 139:13, which maintains that God determines every feature and characteristic of an individual even before conception. (This could lead to the interesting question of how a Christian might feel about cosmetic surgery.) It may be argued that human beings are meddling in matters that belong only to God.

For it was you who created my inward parts; you knit me together in my mother's womb.... My frame was not hidden from you when I was being made in secret, intricately woven in the depths of the earth. Your eyes beheld my unformed substance. In your book were written all the days that were formed for me when none of them yet existed.

(Psalm 139:13,15–16)

One of the major problems raised by genetic engineering is that it also depends on embryo research, and, more recently, on stem cell research. **Stem cells** are the building blocks or master cells of the blood and immune system. Recent work in **cloning** cells has led to the very real possibility of using stem cells to produce healthy genes that can be used to replace defective or unhealthy ones. Stem cells can be used in developing most of the cells within the human body, including heart, blood and brain cells. Stem cells may be taken from unused embryos created for the purpose of IVF, but they can also be taken from a baby's umbilical cord, and from adults. Although adult stem cells are less useful, current research has led scientists to suggest that they may be better than previously thought.

Key words

Cloning
Creating replica cells to replace defective ones or to create new forms of life

Stem cells
Building blocks or master cells of the blood and immune system

Dolly, the world's first cloned sheep

Stem cell research could prove decisive in the development of cures for illnesses such as Alzheimer's disease. However, an obvious fear is that it could lead to cloning — not just human cells but a human being, particularly since work in cloning animals and animal body parts is already advanced. In December 2004 the first fully cloned kitten was developed, at the cost of $50,000, from the DNA of her owner's previous cat who had died the year before. If people are concerned about the moral implications of this, how much more will they be concerned about cloning human beings? Furthermore, is this good use of medical resources and personnel?

Negative eugenics
Using genetic manipulation to remove defective genes, primarily those causing hereditary diseases

Positive eugenics
Using genetic manipulation to improve attributes such as intelligence and personality

Another moral problem raised by genetic engineering is the question of how far humans have the right to replace defective genes (**negative eugenics**). Who decides what is defective or not? Is it good that genetic treatment can lead to the end, in part at least, of genetic diseases such as Huntington's disease, cystic fibrosis and certain forms of cancer? **Positive eugenics** — using genetic engineering to improve intelligence and personality, for example — also raises fears about its potential to change human nature, and, ultimately, the whole community. The information provided by genetic screening, not only in embryos but in adults too, can be used to control the lives of individuals in many ways. Some of these may be good — they provide people with vital information about their genetic makeup, which can guide them in making choices concerning healthcare. However, if employers are able to obtain genetic information about employees, the potential for prejudice is considerable.

Despite the vast amount of research that has taken place into genetic engineering, it is still a developing science. Scientists can only guess at what the long-term consequences may be, and clearly not all of them are good. Furthermore, if anything went wrong with the technology, it could not be corrected. The prospect of human beings who are the product of genetic engineering that has gone wrong is a frightening one.

Religious attitudes to genetic engineering

It may be argued that the positive use of genetic technologies is a good way of fulfilling God's command to be stewards of creation. However, the motives of those who make use of genetic engineering may be at fault. Careful supervision and legislation of the work of genetic scientists might be seen to be the key to making sure that their work remains safe for everyone.

Christian views

Some Christians are opposed to all forms of genetic engineering on the grounds that it takes over God's authority to create life. Furthermore, genetic engineering attempts to perfect human makeup, which is impossible. The earth is not intended to be perfect; only heaven is perfect. Both positive and negative eugenics depend on making judgements about what is considered good or bad, which is worrying for Christians because such judgements are subject to human prejudices and biases. In addition, human beings who were the products of genetic engineering or cloning would be valuable only for what they could do (their instrumental value) — the purpose for which they had been genetically engineered.

Other Christians are more supportive of the principles of genetic engineering on the grounds that Jesus's work in healing people suggests that Christians should do all they can to heal and improve the health of human beings. They do not have an ethical problem with creating cells, and even view research on embryos less than 14 days old as acceptable. However, for Catholics and some other Christians, genetic engineering is only acceptable if it does not involve embryo research, which is against the sanctity of life principle.

Islamic views

Some Muslims accept genetic engineering if it is used to cure disease but not if it is used to create 'perfect' people — the Qur'an and the Hadith teach that Muslims should work to cure sickness. They would accept that genetic engineering of this kind is essentially the same kind of work as developing drugs, and that embryos under 14 days old are not yet foetuses and so can be used for research. Other Muslims, however, oppose all genetic engineering on the grounds that only Allah has the authority to alter someone's genetic structure and it is a haram (forbidden) to take over Allah's authority by this means. Using embryos is the same as abortion, and so Muslim arguments against abortion would be applied in the same way.

Gattaca

The implications of genetic engineering are developed accessibly in the 1997 film, *Gattaca* (15), directed by Andrew Nichol and starring Ethan Hawke and Jude Law. The film opens with a biblical verse running across the screen: 'Consider God's handiwork. Who can straighten what he has made crooked?' (Ecclesiastes 7:13). Although it is a futuristic film, it is set in a 'not too distant future', in which responsible parents do not leave it to God to determine the future of their offspring. Instead, prospective parents ask their local geneticist to engineer a 'perfect' embryo: 'Ten fingers and ten toes —

Vincent uses Jerome's blood, skin and urine samples to enter the space agency

that's all that used to matter. Not now.' The hero of the film, Vincent, was not genetically engineered. He was a 'faith birth' or 'God birth', and, as such, he is destined to be an 'in-valid'. His life expectancy is a mere 30 years, and he suffers from short-sightedness and a heart defect. This genetic make-up determines every choice he has to make and those with imperfect profiles are destined to a life of misery, drifting from one job to another: 'My real résumé was in my cells…. We now have discrimination down to a science.'

His younger brother, Anton, however, is genetically engineered to have 'hazel eyes, dark hair and fair skin' and the geneticist reassures his parents that he has 'eliminated any potentially prejudicial conditions — myopia [short-sightedness], baldness, alcoholism'. When his parents ask whether they should perhaps leave some things to chance, the geneticist advises: 'You want to give your child the best possible start. Believe me, we have enough imperfections built in already. Your child doesn't need any additional burdens.'

While Anton is favoured by his parents, Vincent is brought up to expect very little and his burning ambition to go into space is thwarted at every turn. Working outside the law, he courageously challenges the system and, via a black-market broker of DNA, he enters into a partnership with Jerome Morrow, a former swimming star with 'an IQ off the register…the heart of an ox'. Jerome, however, is in a wheelchair, paralysed by a road accident, bitter and alcoholic. Jerome's fate reveals the real-life tragedies behind the system: 'For the genetically superior, success is easier to obtain, but it is by no means guaranteed. There is no gene for fate, and when the elite fall on hard times, their genetic identity becomes a valuable commodity for the unscrupulous.'

Taking on Jerome's identity, using his blood, urine and skin samples to pass the stringent identity tests, Vincent enters the space agency, Gattaca, and eventually achieves his ambition to be part of a space mission to Titan. Sadly, Jerome commits suicide. He has fulfilled his usefulness in providing Vincent with the means to enter Gattaca, but he has never been able to deal with the 'burden of perfection'. We learn that he had never come to terms with winning only a silver swimming medal, and that his disability was the result of a suicide attempt, not a random car accident.

The question raised by the film is clear: what happens when man takes God's authority to determine life, death and human destiny? Interestingly, both Vincent and Jerome emerge as victims of the system, their future determined by limiting and controlling beliefs about what they should or should not be able to achieve. Neither is free; both are ruled by their genetic profile.

Organ transplantation

Transplant surgery involves using organs from one person, dead or alive, to replace defective or failed organs in someone else. It is an established and advanced form of treatment. However, despite its potential to do enormous good, it has many ethical problems. While **organ transplantation** makes use of organs that would otherwise be wasted and gives people and their relatives the opportunity to offer help to others after their death, it is an expensive and limited form of treatment. It raises

Organ transplant surgery

Key word

Organ transplantation
Using organs from living or dead donors to replace defective organs in other people

important questions about when a person is actually dead, and whether people should be kept alive or allowed to die purely for the purposes of organ donation. Because of the scarcity of organs, other problems arise, not least those raised by the sale of organs from people desperate to raise money, both in the West and in developing countries.

Blood transfusions and bone marrow transplants

Blood transfusions have become a routine medical procedure and in most cultures people give blood free of charge as a gesture of good will. Blood is sorted by blood group and can be stored for when it is needed. Although there are some concerns about the donation of infected blood, this can usually be prevented by screening. Both blood and bone marrow can be donated without permanent loss to the donor. Bone marrow, often used for treating leukaemia, needs to be matched to the patient and close relatives are most likely to provide a match.

Organ donation

Other organs, such as the heart or lung, can only be transplanted from a dead donor or from a live donor if there is a pair (for example, kidneys). In the UK, only genetically related live donors can be used. It is also illegal in the UK to use organs donated as part of a commercial transaction.

Most donated organs come from dead donors. This raises problems as it may be seen to conflict with offering the best available care to the donor patient. It is important that medical teams keep the transplant teams out of the picture until they are certain that the patient is dead. Medical soaps such as *Casualty* or *Holby City* often present dramatic storylines in which patients are kept alive for the purpose of organ donation or where relatives are pressured into making a quick decision about donating the organ of a dying loved one. These issues can be resolved by establishing a clear cause of death. It is therefore normally accepted that death has occurred when the brain stem has died.

In the UK, organ donation is purely voluntary and willingness to donate organs is indicated by carrying an organ donor card or by registering with the NHS Organ Donor Register. However, in some countries the procedure works the other way around, and people must record their wish to opt out of organ donation, otherwise healthy organs are considered freely available

for transplantation and relatives cannot challenge this. In the UK, if an individual does not carry an organ donor card and has not put their name on the donor register, doctors have to ask permission from the next of kin. Most families find some comfort in knowing that their loved one's organs have been used to give life to up to seven different people, but some have ethical or emotional objections to the practice.

In the UK, people willing to donate organs if they die carry an organ donor card

In December 2004, Jorge Miranda, a young American father, began advertising on a billboard in Chicago for a liver donor, using money from an anonymous donor. Three years earlier he had been given 3½ years to live. The advert was written from the point of view of his 5-year-old son, and read: 'My daddy needs a liver'. It featured a family picture, a phone number and a website address (www.mydaddyneedsaliver.com). Although exchanging money

for organs is legal in the USA, advertising for organs is not. The family defended their right to use any means they could to keep Jorge alive, but a transplant specialist criticised the move. He argued that organ donations are allocated on a fair and just system that ensures that those who most need them benefit, and it is ethically questionable whether people should be allowed to bypass the system in this way.

Jorge Miranda and his family appealed online for a liver donor

Non-religious views on organ transplants

One of the major problems facing medical teams making decisions about organ donation is the question of who gets the organ. Should it be the person who has been on the waiting list for a transplant the longest? Or the person with the best tissue match, and therefore the least chance of rejecting the organ? Or the youngest person? Other considerations could be how responsible the medical team feels the patient will be in maintaining their new organ healthily. For example, if there is a likelihood that someone who has received a new liver will drink heavily, should they be allowed to have the transplant? These are difficult judgements to make, particularly when organs are scarce and transplant surgery is expensive.

Another option is the prospect of xenografting — using organs from non-human animals. Some work has been done with chimpanzees, baboons and pigs, but it is a long way from being advanced. Animal organs can carry diseases that would affect humans, and animal rights activists have strong feelings about breeding animals specifically for the purpose of organ donation.

Religious views on organ transplants

Christian views

For most Christians, organ donation is a loving and charitable act and there are no moral problems in receiving a donated organ. There are no implications for life after death since a resurrected body will not need those organs and an immortal soul will not need the body at all. Buying organs from people desperate for money is, however, another matter. This is exploitation, which would be considered wrong by all Christians.

All Christians would be opposed to buying organs from people desperate for money

A person may will to dispose of his body and to destine it to ends that are useful, morally irreproachable and even noble, among them the desire to aid the sick and suffering...this decision should not be condemned but positively justified.

(Pope Pius XII)

Transplants are a great step forward in science's service of man, and not a few people today owe their lives to an organ transplant. Increasingly, the technique of transplants has proven to be a valid

means of attaining the primary goal of all medicine — the service of human life.... There is a need to instil in people's hearts, especially in the hearts of the young, a genuine and deep appreciation of the need for brotherly love, a love that can find expression in the decision to become an organ donor.

(Pope John Paul II)

The donation of organs should be done in a responsible way that reflects loving charity. The Catholic publication, *The Ethical and Religious Directives for Catholic Health Care Services*, lays down a set of principles that clearly explains the use of organ donations. It also states: 'Such organs should not be removed until it has been medically determined that the patient has died. In order to prevent any conflict of interest, the physician who determines death should not be a member of the transplant team.' It also outlines the view that the decision as to who receives organs should be made on medical grounds and not based on age, sex or social status.

The dangers of organ harvesting may be thought to outweigh the benefits

Pope John Paul II observed in *Evangelium Vitae*: 'There is an everyday heroism, made up of gestures and sharing, big or small, which build up an authentic culture of life. A particularly praiseworthy example of such gestures is the donation of organs in a morally acceptable manner.'

Most Protestant Christians believe organ donation is a matter of personal conscience and it is for the individual to make their own free decision. Medical technology, which has made organ and tissue transplants possible, opens up new opportunities for human beings to become partners with God in sustaining and extending the gift of life. There is no direct biblical teaching on organ transplantation, and neither could there be since it was not even a possibility at the time the Bible was written. However, indirect biblical teaching seems to support the principles of love, compassion and sharing that underlie organ donation and transplant. Nevertheless, some Christians argue against the practice on the grounds that it violates the principle of the sanctity of life, mutilating the body and removing what God has given.

Islamic views

Most Muslims object to transplant surgery on the grounds that Shari'ah Law teaches that nothing should be removed from the body after death and that the practice challenges Allah's authority over life and death. The body is sacred and to benefit from the body of any human is sinful. This extends even to the use of hair: 'Allah's curse is on a woman who wears false hair [of humans] or arranges it for others' (Sahih Muslim No. 2122). Deriving benefit from humans can never be justified.

> If a person feared death due to hunger and another person said to him: 'Cut my hand and consume it,' or he said: 'Cut a part of me and eat it,' it will be unlawful for him to do so. Similarly, it is impermissible for a desperate person to cut part of his own self and eat it.
>
> (Fatawa al-Hindiyya, 5/310)

Islam also teaches against the mutilation of the body, although blood transfusions are permitted as long as the body is not mutilated in doing so. Other arguments raised against organ transplantation are that the human body and its organs are owned by Allah and cannot be meddled with by humans, and it is unlawful for individuals to inflict harm upon themselves or others.

Some Muslims have come to accept the practice. The Muslim Law Council of the UK rules that Muslims are permitted to carry donor cards and to receive transplants. It argues that the goal of Islam is to help people by doing good, and transplants offer such an opportunity. Those who support transplants may do so on the grounds that Allah permits some things that would normally be unlawful if they are really necessary, and when a person's life is in danger organ donation would therefore be allowed. It is also argued that organ donation does not violate the sanctity of life or of the body as long as it is done in an appropriate way. Although Allah owns every individual's body, organ donation is as permissible as it would be to risk one's life by entering a burning building to save another person. Furthermore, some argue, since blood transfusions are permissible, there is no reason why other organs should be any different.

Siamese twins

Conjoined twins (**Siamese twins**) originate from a single fertilised egg so they are always identical and same-sex twins. The developing embryo starts to split into identical twins within the first 2 weeks after conception but then stops before completion, leaving a partially separated egg that continues to mature into a conjoined foetus. As a result, cells in Siamese twins become confused about where they are in the body — indeed, which of the two Siamese twins they actually belong to. In normal embryo and foetus development, every cell knows where it is in the body because its neighbours produce chemical messages. So a skin cell knows not only it is skin, but that it is, for example, nose skin rather than chin, ear or lip. In Siamese twins, these chemical messages do not work properly and the end results can be strange, such as a single organism with two heads, two hearts, four legs and arms — or is the single organism actually two individual people?

Siamese twins

Key word

Siamese twins
Conjoined twins created when the developing embryo starts to split into identical twins within the first 2 weeks after conception but stops before completion

In 2000, the case of Siamese twins Mary and Jodie brought the problems of separating such twins to the forefront of the media. Mary and Jodie's parents were told that in order for one twin to live, the other had to die, and if they were not separated, neither would live. Mary was effectively living off Jodie's organs, since hers were so defective. Their parents, devout Catholics, refused to permit an operation, choosing rather to leave the matter in God's hands. However, the case was heard in court and on 22 September the Court of

Appeal decided unanimously that surgery to separate the conjoined twins could go ahead despite the fact that the weaker twin, Mary, would inevitably die. The court observed:

> In a nutshell the problem is this. Jodie and Mary are conjoined twins. They each have their own brain, heart and lungs and other vital organs and they each have arms and legs. They are joined at the lower abdomen. They can be surgically separated. But the operation will kill the weaker twin Mary. This is because her lungs and heart are too deficient to oxygenate and pump blood through her body. Had she been born a singleton, she would not have been viable and resuscitation would have been abandoned. She would have died shortly after her birth. She is alive only because a common artery enables her sister, who is stronger, to circulate life-sustaining oxygenated blood for both of them.
>
> (From 'The Lawfulness of Elective Surgery to Separate Conjoined Twins', the decision of the Court of Appeal (Children), Mary Luckham)

To reach this decision, the court had to decide that Jodie's interests took precedence over Mary's, who was 'designated for death' on the grounds that she was alive only because she drew on Jodie's blood. The actual condition of each twin suggested that Jodie could look forward to the possibility of a good quality of life, but only if separated from Mary, who had no prospect of living independently. Ultimately, the decision was whether it was lawful to kill Mary to save Jodie. The court decided: 'The best interests of the twins is to give the chance of life to the child whose actual bodily condition is capable of accepting the chance to her advantage even if that has to be at the cost of the sacrifice of the life which is so unnaturally supported.'

Religious believers were divided over whether the surgery was morally and ethically right. Many Christians claimed the surgery effectively murdered Mary. Even though it saved Jodie's life, it was a deliberate action that should not be left in human hands, only in God's. However, it could be argued that Mary's death was a secondary effect of saving Jodie's life, which was the primary purpose of the operation. In other words, the intention was not to kill Mary but to save Jodie, although Mary's death was a foreseen outcome of the operation. Other Christians argued it was right to defend Jodie's life because Mary was living on Jodie and neither had the chance of life if left in that condition. Separation was therefore the lesser of the two evils. Some argued that doctors were obliged to use the surgical techniques available to them to separate the twins. Not to do so would have been irresponsible and cruel.

Questions and activities

Sample questions and answers

1 Describe the range of fertility treatments available to infertile couples. (4 marks)

Infertile couples are able to benefit from a range of fertility treatments, most of which must be carried out with the guidance of a fertility specialist. One of the most common is in vitro fertilisation (IVF). In this process, an egg is taken from the mother's womb and is fertilised in a dish using sperm from her partner or a donor, before being replaced in her womb where she carries it to full term. However, some women receive artificial insemination by husband/partner (AIH), in which case the partner's sperm is medically inseminated into the neck of the mother's womb and the woman's egg is fertilised within her body. If a woman's partner is infertile, she may receive artificial insemination by donor (AID), in which the sperm of a donor, usually unknown to the couple, is medically inseminated into her womb. If a woman is herself infertile, she may receive an egg from an anonymous or known donor, which is fertilised with her partner's sperm before being inserted into her womb and carried to full term. In some cases, both sperm and embryo are donated. Perhaps the most controversial method of helping infertile couples is through surrogacy. In gestational surrogacy the egg or sperm (or both) of the couple are fertilised in a dish and then inserted into the womb of another woman, who carries the baby to full term before handing it over to the couple. In traditional surrogacy the surrogate's own egg is used and she may be artificially inseminated with the father's sperm. In the most extreme case, the surrogate may conceive through sexual intercourse with the father, having agreed to carry the child on behalf of the father and his own partner and to hand it over to them after birth.

2 Give an outline of different Christian attitudes to fertility treatment. (4 marks)

Because much fertility treatment involves the use of embryo research, some Christians, particularly Catholics and Evangelicals, are opposed to it. Embryo research makes use of embryos younger than 14 days old, which may be products themselves of fertility treatment, or may have been created in vitro for the purpose of embryo research. Christians who believe these embryos are fully human on the grounds that life begins at conception argue that to carry out research on them is morally wrong and violates the sanctity of life. They may also argue that fertility treatment is, in itself, wrong, because those who are infertile should accept it as God's will for them and seek other ways in which God may be calling them to his service as a childless couple.

However, other more liberal Christians may argue that fertility treatment simply makes use of divinely given gifts. God has given humans the ability to use medical technology for a range of beneficial purposes, and fertility treatment is one such legitimate means. Furthermore, they may claim that having children is a joy that God would not deny people if there were means to make this possible. They may still argue, however, that there are some methods of fertility treatment that are more acceptable than others. Using sperm or eggs from an anonymous donor may be thought to break the 'one flesh' principle between husband and wife, and surrogacy presents even more problems, not least if the mother decides not to hand over the child once it is born. Almost all Christians would argue that adoption is a good way of dealing with infertility because it not only benefits the adoptive parents but expresses God's love to others in need at the same time.

3 Explain the different views of religious believers concerning organ donation. (8 marks)

Some Muslims believe that as the goal of Islam is to help people by doing good, organ transplants offer such an opportunity. Allah permits some things that would normally be unlawful if necessity dictates it, and when someone's life is in danger, organ transplantation should be allowed if it is done in an appropriate way. Blood transfusions are permissible, so some Muslims argue that the donation of other organs should not be any different.

However, other Muslims disagree on the grounds that Shari'ah Law teaches that nothing should be removed from the body after death. Because the body is sacred, to benefit from the body of any human is sinful and can never be justified: 'If a person feared death due to hunger and another person said to him: "Cut my hand and consume it," or he said: "Cut a part of me and eat it," it will be unlawful for him to do so. Similarly, it is impermissible for a desperate person to cut part of his own self and eat it' (Fatawa al-Hindiyya, 5/310). Some Muslims may therefore argue that the human body and its organs are owned by Allah and so cannot be meddled with by humans.

For most Christians, organ donation is a loving and charitable act and there are no moral problems in receiving a donated organ. There are no implications for life after death because a resurrected body will not need those organs and an immortal soul will not need the body at all. Buying organs from people desperate for money is, however, another matter. This is exploitation, which would be considered wrong by all Christians. This is supported by the teaching of Pope John Paul II in *Evangelium Vitae*, who claimed: 'There is an everyday heroism, made up of gestures and sharing, big or small, which build up an authentic culture of life. A particularly praiseworthy example of such gestures is the donation of organs in a morally acceptable manner.'

4 'Genetic engineering should be left to God, not to humans.' Do you agree? Give reasons for your opinion, showing you have considered other points of view. In your answer, you should refer to religion. (8 marks)

Genetic engineering poses difficulties for Christians because of the methods it uses and the possible outcome of its use. The use of embryos and stem cells in genetic research is a major problem for conservative, Evangelical and Catholic Christians, who argue that it breaks the principle of the sanctity of life to use embryos for this purpose. However, the possible consequences of genetic engineering present unique problems. In Genesis and in the Psalms, it is made clear that creation is the work of God alone and that he has special plans and purposes for those whom he creates in his image. Genetic engineering involves the manipulation of genes to change the genetic structure of human beings, either by enhancing positive characteristics or by removing defective ones. Either way, this changes the human being from God's initial creative design, and may suggest that humans think they know better than God.

Difficulties arise when humans try to decide what they think is genetically good, and worth enhancing, or genetically bad, and therefore should be eliminated. While most would agree that it is good to remove genetic diseases, is it good to eliminate characteristics such as baldness or short sight, or is some element of diversity in these matters good among human beings? Is it good to enhance qualities such as intelligence or strength? While it may seem to be so at face value, Christians may worry that if human beings are created purposely for these reasons, we will stop valuing people for themselves and value them for what they can do.

On the other hand, many Christians may argue that Jesus's work on earth was spent in healing and improving the lives of human beings. Therefore, genetic engineering is a legitimate extension of that work. Christians are called to do whatever they can to heal and to promote health, so as long as the means used do not violate the fundamental principles of the sanctity of life, they should be pursued.

Class activities and homework

Understanding fertility treatment

Your teacher will choose two people from your class to represent a childless couple which is desperate to have IVF, and two people to represent two religious believers who are opposed to fertility treatment. Each pair should spend 10 minutes working out the arguments they are going to use to persuade the rest of the class to vote in their favour. Your teacher will guide the pairs in presenting their arguments to the class. After all the arguments have been made, cast a vote on the basis of the evidence presented. Will you grant these parents their wish, or will you side with their opponents? When the votes have been cast, your teacher will ask several of you how you reached your decision. Which arguments persuaded you and why?

'Childless people should accept God's will and use their other gifts in his service.'
'A loving God would never expect a childless couple to suffer unnecessarily.'
In the light of your debate in class, compare and contrast these two statements, using all the arguments you and your classmates have raised.

Understanding genetic engineering

As a class, watch the film *Gattaca*. In the next lesson, your teacher will guide you in producing a mindmap identifying the moral problems that arise from the film. You may like to use the following headings to organise your thoughts:

- The immediate problems posed by the practice of genetic engineering: for example, who controls it? who decides what are desirable and un-desirable characteristics?
- Issues of discrimination: for example, what happens to those who are not genetically engineered?
- Issues of freedom and potential: for example, should people be compelled to follow the lifestyle chosen for them by their parents or the geneticist?
- Issues for society: for example, is there any room for spirituality or religion in the Gattaca society?

Use the internet to find out about the making of the film *Gattaca* and the use of symbolism and other devices to convey its message. For example, the letters in Gattaca come from the four chemicals that determine the genetic material of an individual. Prepare a fact sheet on your research and share your views with the rest of the class.

Understanding transplant surgery

Your teacher will divide the class into pairs. In each pair, one of you should be a patient who needs a transplant and one of you should be the patient's doctor. Present a case as to why you or your patient should be the one to receive a single kidney that has become available. Under your teacher's guidance, present your case to the rest of the class. After every pair has argued their case, your teacher, as the hospital administrator, will say who will receive the kidney and why.

'The separation of Siamese twins as soon as possible after birth, whatever the risks, should be compulsory.' Do you agree? Give reasons for your opinion, showing you have considered another point of view. In your answer, you should refer to religion.

Religion and science

Religious teachings on cosmology

Christian interpretations

> The universe was formed at God's command, so that what is seen was not made out of what was visible.
>
> (Hebrews 11:3)

Key word

Cosmology
The study of how the universe came into existence

Cosmology is the study of how the universe came into existence. It is of interest to both scientists and religious believers, although each group traditionally has been thought of as approaching the subject in different ways.

Religious teachings about the responsibility of stewardship are based on the belief that God created the world and gave human beings the task of keeping and looking after it. Thus, beliefs about the environment and the relationship humans are expected to have with it are linked to beliefs about how the world came to be. Most religious believers maintain that God created the earth, although the length of time he took over this varies among different religious groups. The most traditional views shared by Christianity and Judaism are based on the creation narrative of Genesis 1 and 2.

Genesis 1 and 2 relate two different accounts of creation. In Genesis 1, God's creative activity is broken up over 7 days, and the seventh is a day when God rests and reflects on his handiwork.

- Day one: the first act of creation is light.
- Day two: the sky is created, described as a dome to separate the water under it from that above it.
- Day three: water is gathered together to form the oceans, and land and vegetation appear.
- Day four: lights in the sky are created — sun, moon and stars.
- Day five: sea creatures and birds are created.
- Day six: animal life is created, and, finally, humans.
- Day seven: having finished his work, God rests and is pleased with all he has made. It is described as 'very good'.

In Genesis 2, heaven and earth are formed, then Adam, the first man, from the dust of the ground and by the breath of God, then the trees, vegetation, birds and animals, and, finally, Eve is made from Adam's rib. The account of Genesis 2 is linked with that of temptation and the Fall in Genesis 3, and certain features of creation — such as the tree of the knowledge of good and evil and God's forbidding humans to eat fruit from it — are included in Genesis 2. The accounts in Genesis 1 and 2 share common themes.

Part of the depiction of the creation by Michelangelo on the ceiling of the Sistine Chapel

- God alone is responsible for creating the world.
- Humans have a special place in creation.
- God's creative work is perfect and purposeful.
- There is a perfect relationship between all parts of creation, which support each other.
- Human beings are given special responsibilities.

However, not all Christians agree on exactly how these narratives are meant to be interpreted. Some believe that the Bible was written by God and that every word is literally true. Others believe that the Bible was written by people who were influenced by God, but that not every word is literally true.

The differences between these approaches are important, since they influence the way in which religious believers approach the whole Bible. If the creation accounts are intended to be taken literally, very real challenges are posed by scientific explanations of how the universe was formed. If, on the other hand, they are just myths or stories, they may still contain important religious truths. It is possible that religious and scientific accounts might actually help each other.

Islamic interpretations

Islam does not have a specific story about how the universe was created, although the Qur'an makes several references to Allah's creation of heaven, earth, Adam, Eve and Iblis (Satan).

> Behold, thy Lord said to the angels: 'I will create a vice regent on earth.' They said, 'Wilt thou place therein one who will make mischief therein and shed blood, whilst we do celebrate thy praises and glorify thy holy name?'
>
> (Surah 2:31)

> O mankind! Reverence your guardian-Lord, who created you from a single person, created, of like nature, his mate, and from the two of them scattered (like seeds) countless men and women.
>
> (Surah 4:1)

> Your guardian-Lord is Allah, who created the heavens and earth in six days, and is firmly established on the throne of authority....

He created the sun, the moon, the stars, all governed by laws under
his command. Is it not his to create and to govern? Blessed be Allah,
the Cherisher and Sustainer of the world!

(Surah 7:54)

Islam shares a number of similarities with Christianity in its teaching about
creation, including the role of Adam and Eve from whom all humans are
believed to be descended and who take responsibility for humanity's fall
from God's favour in the garden of Eden. As with Christianity, there are traditional and modern views. Traditional teaching accepts the literal truth of the
Qur'an that Allah created the universe in 6 days and that Adam and Eve were
the first humans. The modern view, associated with Islamic scientists such
as Dr Maurice Bucaille, suggests that the Arabic of the Qur'an indicates
six ages of creation, not 6 days, and highlights the lack of a creative order
in the Qur'an. Over the six ages, God created the universe, life on earth, and
then humans, an order that fits an evolutionary process. Through the creation of scientific laws, Allah made possible the creation of the universe and
life, and intervened specifically in the creation of humans by breathing life
into them.

The Qur'an shows the evolution of the heavens and the earth. It
speaks of an original gaseous mass, which split to form the universe.

(Dr Maurice Bucaille, *The Qur'an and Modern Science*)

What is a religious interpretation of the universe?

It is clear that a religious interpretation of the origin of the world and of
human beings does not depend on a literal interpretation of religious texts.
Some religious believers maintain this is vital, but many others do not,
although they still argue that God was directly involved. There are five important features about the religious view of creation:

- The facts of creation cannot be fully explained without reference to God.
- God created something out of nothing (creation *ex nihilo*).
- Creation is the result of God's actions.
- Creation reflects God's nature and his purpose for the universe and
  humans.
- No single religious explanation exists.

Problems with creation cosmologies

One of the major problems posed by the creation stories is that they are read as if they are supposed to be scientific accounts. It is important to remember that they were written thousands of years ago, before scientific discoveries of the sort that are now taken for granted were even thought possible. The purpose of biblical and Qur'anic writers was not to write a literally true, scientifically factual account, but rather to express beliefs they had about the relationship between God and the world. The writers believed that God was involved in the creation of the world, but they could not possibly know exactly how it came about. The narratives convey beliefs about God that are put into story form to make them easier to grasp.

Interestingly, the Genesis accounts do not seem to be trying to explain how the earth was made, but rather to describe how God gave life to a dead planet: 'In the beginning, when God created the universe, the earth was without form and void and darkness covered the whole earth, while the spirit of God swept over the face of the waters' (Genesis 1:1–2). It is possible to say that scientific theories about the universe coming about through an enormous explosion may be correct without saying that the biblical accounts are wrong.

God created something out of nothing

One of the biggest problems of the biblical accounts is the 6-day process of creation. The word 'day' is now thought to be just a useful term for a period of time. Furthermore, the order in which things were created is in line with a scientific explanation. The main purpose of the stories, therefore, is likely to be to emphasise the design of the world and the fact that humans were created to look after it.

Scientific cosmologies

The two major scientific interpretations of how the earth, humans and animal life came into existence are natural selection and evolution, and the Big Bang.

Charles Darwin's theory of evolution by natural selection

In order to survive, animals have to change to suit their living conditions. Each new generation of animals is born slightly more suited to the conditions and can live better in them.

Although Darwin's intention was not to challenge religious beliefs, many Christians were shocked by his theories. They not only seemed to do away with the need for a God, but they traced human origins back to more primitive forms of life. This seemed to go against the belief that humans were created for a special relationship with God.

Charles Darwin

The Big Bang

This is the theory that some 15 billion years ago a tremendous explosion started the universe. Our own solar system, including the earth, is thought to be around 4.6 million years old, and humans are thought to have evolved around 2.5 million years ago. At the time of the Big Bang, all of the matter and energy of space was contained at one point. What existed prior to this event is completely unknown. This was not an ordinary explosion, but an event filling all of space as all the particles of the new universe rushed away from each other. The Big Bang consisted of an explosion of space within itself, unlike an explosion of a bomb in which fragments are thrown outwards. The galaxies were not all clumped together, but rather the Big Bang laid the foundations of the universe. After the Big Bang, when the earth had cooled, life began to develop — sea and land vegetation, single-celled marine creatures, land and water dwellers, dinosaurs, mammals, and, ultimately, humans.

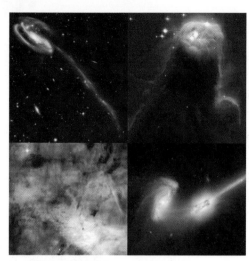

Images from the Hubble space telescope

Enormously powerful telescopes have made it possible to track stars billions of kilometres away, the light from which takes thousands of years to reach earth. It is possible, therefore, that light deep in space from the original Big Bang can still be seen.

A purely scientific interpretation of the origin of the universe and life is based on the following principles:

- God did not create it.
- The universe has no meaning.
- The universe is not designed.

Are science and religion connected?

The big question is how science and religion are connected, if they are at all. Finding connections between religion and science raises six problems which require solutions.

The problems

Interpretation

Science and religion are faced with the same data — such as fossils, variety of species, the structure of human bodies, DNA — but their significance may be interpreted differently. Those who reject a religious interpretation of the data often do so because they believe religion does not explain them adequately. Richard Dawkins argues that: 'Religion is no longer a serious candidate in the field of explanation. It is completely superseded by science' (quoted in John Blanchard, *Does God Believe in Atheists?* 2000).

Language and style

Religion uses myths, stories and symbols. Science deals with literal fact; religion is like poetry. Richard Dawkins claims that the creation narratives of the Bible have 'no more status than hundreds, thousands of creation myths around the world.'

How versus why

Is science concerned with the way the universe works and religion with the meaning of it? If this is the case, people cannot expect to find religion answering questions about how the universe came into existence, or science answering questions about what it all means. However, this has not stopped scientists and religious believers attempting to cross over, and in 1625 Archbishop James Usher estimated, on the basis of Old Testament data, that God created the universe at 9 a.m. on 24 October 4004 BCE.

Purpose versus meaninglessness

Does the religious believer seek meaning, purpose and a goal to the universe while the scientist sees it as ultimately meaningless? Richard Dawkins argues that the purpose of the universe and human existence is answered by humans themselves. He does not allow religion, however, to have anything to contribute to the search for meaning: 'What has theology ever said that is of the smallest use to anybody? The achievements of theologians don't do anything, don't affect anything, don't achieve anything, don't even mean anything. What makes you think that theology is a subject at all?'

Richard Dawkins

The nature of human significance

Do religious believers feel that there is a special significance for humanity while scientists interpret humanity as nothing more than the species at the top of the evolutionary chain? Again, Richard Dawkins suggests that human purpose is the result of humans having broken Darwin's laws so that they no longer need to concentrate on survival alone. Humans can communicate, think ahead, plan and create things at a speed that takes them beyond the speed of biological evolution. Humans, therefore, create their own significance because their brains have developed fast enough to enable them to do so.

Scientific 'fact' versus religious 'opinion'

Scientists make judgements and draw conclusions on the basis of what they currently know but which may change in the future, possibly because they gain more information. Any scientific explanation about the origins of the universe is therefore open to change. For example, it was once thought that the world was flat — we now know otherwise.

Some scientists suggest that Darwin's theories are merely an idea that may change. Darwin himself recognised that there were flaws in this theory and that it was based on his best judgement at the time:

> A crowd of difficulties will have occurred to the reader. Some of them are so grave that to this day I can never reflect on them without being staggered, but, to the best of my judgement, the greater number are only apparent; and those that are real are not, I think, fatal to my theory.
>
> (Quoted in Michael Banner, *The Justification of Science and the Rationality of Religious Belief*, 1990)

Religious views, however, may be considered by some scientists to be value-less. Richard Dawkins argues: 'Faith is the great cop-out, the excuse to avoid the need to think and to evaluate evidence.' He claims that it is so important to find an explanation for the universe that human beings should never be satisfied with supernatural explanations, which he considers to be non-explanations.

The solutions

There are a number of possible answers to these problems. For instance, we could say that:

- Scientific explanations are wrong; religious explanations are right.
- Religious explanations are wrong; scientific explanations are right. Religious explanations belong to the 'pre-scientific' age before science had been accepted widely.
- Both explanations are correct in their own way — the environment in which they are used and the people who use them understand each other and what they mean. According to this view, scientific explanations of the world are meaningful, relevant and understandable to people who work with science and who agree this is the way they are going to look at the world. Religious views of the origins of the world are understood by people who think religiously about them. They are both true within the circles in

which they are used. This approach is sometimes called language games, and is associated with the twentieth-century Austrian philosopher, Ludwig Wittgenstein. He said of language: 'Don't ask for the meaning, look for the use.' By this principle, scientific claims belong to their area of life and are used correctly or incorrectly within their language game, and religious views within theirs, so neither believer nor scientist is in a position to criticise the other because they are not playing the same game by the same rules.

Ludwig Wittgenstein

Other issues

For many religious believers, religion and science are both right. The Big Bang, natural selection and **evolutionism** are the tools that God has used to bring the universe, animal and human life into being. It seems logical that God should give his creation some freedom by allowing it to evolve rather than creating it fully formed and unable to change. Furthermore, it is more in line with God's sustaining and caring for his creation that this process should continue over many millions of years than that it should happen in a single burst of activity by a God who then appears to do nothing.

> **Key word**
>
> **Evolutionism**
> The view that the universe and life came about through a chemical and biological process over billions of years

One of the biggest conflicts between religion and science has been whether it is possible that the universe came about by chance. Traditionally, religious believers have suggested that the conditions necessary for life are too complex to have come about randomly — a probability comparable to a hurricane blowing through a scrap yard and assembling a Boeing 747.

> Even if the whole universe consisted of organic soup, the chance of producing the basic enzymes of life by random processes without intelligent direction would be approximately one in 10 with 40,000 zeroes after it....

A Boeing 747–400 has 6 million parts

Darwinian evolution is most unlikely to get even one polypeptide right, let alone the thousands on which living cells depend for survival.

(Dave Hunt, *In Defence of the Faith*, 1996)

On the other hand, scientists, such as Peter Atkins, have claimed that it is not unreasonable to speak of the universe coming about by chance: 'We can even begin to discern how the universe could come from absolute nothing as time induced (by chance) its own existence' (quoted in John Blanchard, *Does God Believe in Atheists?* 2000). The idea that people could speak of the universe having no explanation other than chance — a non-explanation — has been opposed by religious thinkers such as Keith Ward, who claims: 'Science is based on the postulate that one should always seek reasons for why things are as they are.... If I ask "Why does water boil as it is heated?" I do not expect to be told, "There is no reason at all. It just does"' (op. cit.).

However, it is possible that both science and religion could agree on the need for an explanation of the universe and human life. Richard Dawkins argues that the notion of life coming about by one single chance is unreasonable, but for it to be the product of a series of chances is another, more likely, matter. Dawkins stops a long way short of suggesting that God is the author of any of those chances, but for many religious believers — scientists and non-scientists — God is the most reasonable and most likely explanation. Richard Swinburne argues that God is a vital explanation for the universe:

So there is our universe. It is characterised by vast, all persuasive temporal order, the conformity of nature to formula, recorded in the scientific laws formulated by humans. It started off in such a way...as to lead to the evolution of animals and humans. These phenomena are clearly things too big for science to explain.... Note that I am not postulating a 'God of the gaps', a god merely to explain the things which science has not yet explained. I am postulating a God to explain what science explains; I do not deny that science explains, but I postulate God to explain why science explains.

(Richard Swinburne, *Is There a God?* 1996)

Some scientists who have a religious faith have started to observe that science cannot provide all the answers about the creation and development of the universe and its species. Science may be able to guide people towards some answers, but many scientists themselves have claimed that what science has discovered itself needs an explanation, which science cannot provide. Josh McDowall observes: 'Oddly enough, of all the worlds in collision today, it is the scientific world that is increasingly giving the greatest and most shocking evidence in favour of God's existence' (Josh McDowall, *New Evidence That Demands a Verdict*, 1999). He quotes Stephen Hawking's *A Brief History of Time* (1988):

> The initial state of the universe must have been very carefully chosen indeed if the hot big bang model was correct right back to the beginning of time. It would be very difficult to explain why the universe should have begun in just this way, except as an act of God who intended to create beings like us.

Stephen Hawking

Landmarks in the science and religion debate

1860 During the Oxford evolution debate, Bishop Wilberforce asked T. H. Huxley, Darwin's public defender, whether it was on his grandmother's or his grandfather's side that he was descended from an ape. Huxley replied that he would prefer to be descended from an ape than from a person like the bishop, who treated such serious ideas so casually.

1925 In Dayton, Tennessee, a biology teacher, John Scopes, was prosecuted and fined by the state of Tennessee for teaching Darwin's theory of evolution, previously banned by the state legislature because it conflicted with the account of the creation in Genesis.

1982 The Arkansas state legislature passed a law that required the equal treatment in schools of evolution and creationism. The judge ruled that because creationism is not a science (it cannot be falsified), it cannot be taught as part of the science curriculum in the same way as evolutionary theories.

1995–86 Five American states passed similar legislation to the Arkansas legislation of 1982.

Questions and activities

Sample questions and answers

1 Outline the Christian cosmology.   (4 marks)

Christian cosmology is based on the teaching of Genesis 1 and 2, which describes God's creation of the universe, animal and human life. The two accounts are different in structure and yet contain many similar features. In Genesis 1, God creates the universe in 6 days, resting on the seventh day, while in Genesis 2 there is no suggestion of how long he took, and the way in which he created human beings is different. In Genesis 1, humans are created in the image of God after everything else has been created, so they are the climax of God's creation. In Genesis 2, their important role is shown by creating Adam first, out of the dust of the earth and the breath of God, and Eve at the end of the process, completing it by providing man with an appropriate partner to share responsibility for creation.

God creates *ex nihilo* (out of nothing) in both accounts, and in Genesis 1 the power of his word to bring things into being is emphasised. Everything is created in a logical order, starting with light and water before vegetation, sea and land creatures, and, finally, humans. When everything is complete, God judges it to be 'very good' — in other words, it is perfect. Genesis 2 connects creation with the events that lead up to the Fall in Genesis 3 — the tree of the knowledge of good and evil in the centre of the garden, and the command to man and woman not to eat of it. This suggests that the perfection of God's creation was spoiled because humans were disobedient.

In both accounts, God alone is responsible for bringing something out of nothing and order out of chaos. Humans have a special place and special responsibilities in creation, whether they were created first or last. God's creative work is perfect and has a purpose, and all things relate together harmoniously.

2 Explain the reasons why scientific cosmologies are sometimes seen as contradicting religious explanations of the universe.
                    (8 marks)

The two prevailing scientific cosmologies — the Big Bang and the theory of evolution — are often seen as contradicting religious cosmologies because they identify ways in which the universe and life could have come about without reference to God. Scientific cosmologies essentially maintain that the universe came about without any personal direction or intelligent design and that it has no metaphysical purpose or meaning. There was no supernatural intervention involved in the forming of the universe, which is the result of independent physical, chemical and biological processes.

Charles Darwin's theory of evolution by natural selection claims that because of competition for food, the young of any species compete for survival. Those who survive to produce the next generation have favourable natural variations that are passed on by natural selection. Each generation may improve adaptively over the preceding generations, and this gradual and continual process is the source of evolution of the species. Darwinists suggest that all related organisms are descended from common ancestors and that the earth itself is not static but evolving.

Although Darwin's intention was not to challenge religious belief, many Victorian Christians were shocked by his theories, which not only seemed to do away with the need for a divine creator, but traced human origins back to more primitive forms of life. This seemed to go against the belief that humans were created for a special relationship with God.

The Big Bang theory claims that 15 billion years ago a tremendous explosion started the expansion of the universe. Our own solar system, including the earth, is thought to be around 4.6 million years old, and humans are thought to have evolved around 2.5 million years ago. The Big Bang was an event that filled all of space as particles rushed away from each other and laid the foundations of the universe. After the Big Bang, when the earth had cooled, life began to develop — sea and land vegetation, single-celled marine creatures, land and water dwellers, dinosaurs, their land-dwelling and sea-dwelling descendants, and, ultimately, humans. This theory can be seen to contradict religious cosmology as it is a completely impersonal event that happened by chance. There is nothing special about its outcome, since there was no personal intention involved.

3 'It is a contradiction to be a scientist and to be religious.' Do you agree? Give reasons for your opinion, showing you have considered other points of view. (8 marks)

I believe that it is impossible to be a scientist and to be religious if as a religious believer you accept only a literal interpretation of Genesis, called creationism.

To maintain that the universe and life were created *ex nihilo* by the word of God in 6 days is not compatible with scientific discoveries that have become well known since the nineteenth century. Creationism is not a science because it cannot be proved true or false by scientific means. In 1925, Tennessee biology teacher John Scopes was prosecuted and fined by the state of Tennessee for teaching Darwin's theory of evolution, previously banned by the state because it conflicted with the account of the creation in Genesis, making a clear public statement that one could either be a scientist and teach evolution or a religious believer and accept creationism. Teaching evolution was effectively seen as opposing religious cosmology.

Richard Dawkins argues that it is impossible to be a scientist and a religious believer because he thinks religious interpretations of the world are mentally degrading. He suggests that people who are satisfied with a religious explanation are accepting a non-explanation because it stops them from discovering more about the world, which is the scientist's task. Dawkins believes human beings hold the key to discovering everything there is to know about the world, but only by using scientific methods, not by holding religious beliefs.

However, I believe it is possible to be a scientist and to be religious if you see scientific discoveries as revealing more about God's creation and the nature of the universe and human life. Religious belief could be seen to add to the scientists' investigations because they bring an extra dimension to their work. Religious belief adds a sense of wonder to the discoveries of science and science explains something about the purpose and meaning of the universe — it does not just provide mechanical, impersonal answers about how the universe came to be. Dennis Alexander, a world-renowned immunologist and also a Christian, argues that while as a biologist he uses evolution as the starting point of any investigation and experimentation, he sees it as perfectly logical that evolution would be the tool that God used to bring about life. He suggests that Dawkins's approach leads to a life without meaning because it is a life of atheism.

Class activities and homework

Understanding religious cosmologies

In small groups, divide a large sheet of paper into six columns, using both sides if necessary, and label each column Day 1, Day 2, and so on. In the relevant column, write what Genesis 1 describes as being created on that day, and then add verse references from Genesis 2 that indicate when, according to that account, the same features were created. Add verses from the Qur'an under the relevant days to show the connections between the two religious cosmologies. Finally, in each column add a reference from elsewhere in the Bible that describes God's act of creation. For example, in the Day 2 column, you could add Psalm 104:6.

Using the internet or other resources, find out about the cosmology of a non-monotheistic religion. Share your research with the rest of the class.

Understanding scientific cosmologies

Your teacher will provide you with some notes about the work of important scientific discoveries over the centuries that have posed challenges to traditional religious beliefs — for example, the work of Copernicus and Galileo. As a class, discuss the reasons why it was considered important that these discoveries were brought into the open despite the conflicts that arose.

'Scientific discoveries about the world are far more important to the development of humanity than learning about religion.' Do you agree? Give reasons for your opinion, showing you have considered other points of view.

Understanding the connections between science and religion

Go back to the table you made linking the events of Genesis 1 and 2 with other references to God's creation in the Bible. Either on another table or, if you have room, on the same sheet, identify ways in which scientific cosmologies might be compatible with what is described in Genesis or elsewhere in the Bible. Make sure you use at least two scholars or scientists and quotations from them.

'Scientific discoveries make religious beliefs about the universe more, not less, amazing.' Do you agree? Give reasons for your opinion, showing you have considered other points of view.

Glossary

Acid rain Burning fossil fuels generates sulphuric acid and nitric acid, which make rain more acidic. This affects vegetation and buildings

Adoption A legally binding relationship between a couple and a child to whom they are not biologically related

Animal rights The principle that animals have the right not to be exploited by human beings

Bible The holy book of Christianity

Bullying Hurting, frightening, intimidating or humiliating another person

Cabinet The group of senior ministers who help the prime minister make important decisions concerning the running of the country

Capital punishment The death penalty

Church The Christian community. It is also used to refer to a Christian place of worship

Cloning Creating replica cells to replace defective ones or to create new forms of life

Conscience The part of the mind where a sense of right and wrong is developed

Conservation Preserving and protecting the environment and its natural resources

Cosmology The study of how the universe came into existence

Creation God making the earth out of nothing

Crime An action that is against the criminal law

Decalogue The Ten Commandments, found in Exodus 20 in the Bible

Democracy A society that has free elections and gives all its citizens the chance to vote on who they want to govern them

Deterrence Making punishments so severe that people will be put off (deterred) from committing crimes

Electoral system The way in which voting at an election is organised

Embryology Medical research using embryos

Evolutionism The view that the universe and life came about through a chemical and biological process over billions of years

Faith without works The idea that having religious faith on its own is not enough and it needs to be accompanied by good works

Fertility treatment Using medical technology to conceive a child

First-past-the-post The voting system used in the UK to decide who is elected to be the member of parliament for each constituency. The winner is the person with the most votes

Forgiveness Ending a dispute with someone and not blaming them for what has gone wrong

Genetic engineering Changing the gene structure, primarily to cure genetically inherited diseases by modifying affected genes

Global warming Increased carbon dioxide in the atmosphere raises the temperature of the earth, with potentially devastating effects on the environment

Golden Rule Jesus's teaching that people should treat other people in the same way they themselves would like to be treated

Halal The Islamic practice of slaughtering animals in a permissible, humane manner

Infertility Being unable to conceive a child naturally

Judgement The act of weighing up and assessing what people have done and what punishments, if any, should be enforced

Justice Maintaining what is fair, right and equal to all

Just war The basis upon which a Christian can decide when it is right to go to war. It refers to a war that is fought in a right way and for the right reasons

Khalifah The Islamic principle that humans have a responsibility to act as Allah's representatives on earth

Law The rules that govern the smooth-running of human relationships in society

Local government Government at a local level. This refers to local, district and parish councils which are responsible for local matters such as education

National government The government of the whole country, led by the prime minister

Natural resources Natural products and environments that are used by humans — coal, oil, fertile land and gas, for example

Negative eugenics Using genetic manipulation to remove defective genes, primarily those causing hereditary diseases

Non-renewable resources Natural resources which cannot be replaced, such as coal

Nuclear weapons Weapons such as atomic bombs, which are based on atomic fission or fusion

Organ transplantation Using organs from living or dead donors to replace defective organs in other people

Pacifism Refusing to fight in a war

Pollution The contamination of the natural environment

Positive eugenics Using genetic manipulation to improve attributes such as intelligence and personality

Proportional representation The voting system that looks at the proportion of votes each party gets and distributes seats in line with that percentage. For example, a party with 25% of the votes gets 25% of the seats

Punishment The penalty for committing an offence

Reconciliation Bringing people back together after a dispute

Reform Using punishment to help people not to offend again and helping them to become law-abiding members of society

Renewable resources Natural resources which can be renewed by replanting, such as trees, or which replenish themselves, such as sunshine

Retribution Using punishment to make criminals suffer and pay for the wrong they have done

Siamese twins Conjoined twins created when the developing embryo starts to split into identical twins within the first 2 weeks after conception but stops before completion

Situation ethics A method of deciding right from wrong by considering what is the most loving thing to do

Stem cells Building blocks or master cells of the blood and immune system

Stewardship Taking care of the environment on behalf of God and for the benefit of future generations

Weapons of mass destruction Chemical, biological and nuclear weapons that can devastate large areas and kill huge numbers of people. Examples include poison gas, anthrax and smallpox

Welfare State A system whereby the government ensures that the basic needs of the poorest members of society are met

World peace Removing the causes of war so that everyone lives in safety

Useful websites

Islam

These websites provide answers to questions about Islam, Islamic–Christian relations, and Islamic responses to world and social issues:

www.answering-islam.org.uk   www.islam101.com   www.islamonline.net

Religious, ethical and cultural issues in the media

The BBC website features regularly changing articles on religious and ethical issues in the news: www.bbc.co.uk/religion

Channel 4's webpage on religious and cultural issues is linked to relevant programmes on its network: www.channel4.com/culture

Science and religion

www.answersingenesis.org

Charities

www.cafod.org.uk   www.care.orq.uk   www.christian-aid.org.uk
www.muslimaid.org

Bullying

www.childline.org.uk   www.dfes.gov.uk/bullying   www.kidscape.org.uk

Revision

The BBC GCSE Bitesize website is focused on revision. It contains summaries of key topics and practice tests:

www.bbc.co.uk/schools/gcsebitesize/re

These websites contain articles on Christian philosophy and ethics which are useful for revision:

www.beliefnet.com   www.christiantopics.com   www.faithnet.org

Index

A

B

C

D

E

S

T

U

V

W

Z